My Healing Belongs to Me, by Steve Long, and desire to see you healed. The stories and testimonies along with scriptural references are uplifting. This is a great book to encourage those who need healing, including those who don't know Jesus. I highly recommend that you buy several copies and give them away!

—DR. CHÉ AHN Apostle, *Harvest Apostolic Center*; Apostolic Leader, *HRock Church*, Pasadena, CA; President, *Harvest International Ministry*; International Chancellor, *Wagner Leadership Institute*

After many years of knowing Steve and being involved with his ministry, we appreciate the encouragement he gives to so many wanting to grow in their faith for healing and the love of God. Filled with personal stories of the miraculous, this book will encourage you and increase your faith for healing in your own life and the lives of others.

—ROLLAND & HEIDI BAKER Founders and Directors of *Iris Global*

Can you as a Christian pray for healing? Should you as a Christian pray for healing? Steve Long takes us on his personal journey in answer to these questions. Walk with Steve and you will find that God's heart is that all would be healed. This healing truly belongs to you!

—RALPH A. BEISNER Pastor, Author, Lawyer, Retired New York State Justice

Steve Long has ministered with his wife Sandra at our church in Summerside P.E.I. and we saw many healings during their stay with us. This book is simply exceptional on so many levels. Firstly it is biblically supported at every step and is full of small tips taking the mystery out of 'healing ministry.' I love the way Steve gives so many illustrations of how everyone gets to play and participate in healing. Ministry is not simply for the platform guests and this book makes that point over and over. God wants to use you to heal and this book will wet your appetite for more. 'Not only did Jesus minister out of his humanity but he expects us to do the same.' In fact, I could re-read this book simply to be encouraged by the stories in themselves.

—ANDREW BRYCE Pastor of *Sunnyside Community Church*, P.E.I.

It is a very great honour to recommend to you this outstanding book, *My Healing Belongs To Me*, by Pastor Steve Long. Steve has an incredible "charism" that is currently essential in the Body of Christ at large. As Roman Catholics, we often struggle with the questions of whether God wants to heal us or not, whether we should be carrying this burden or pain, and identifying with the sufferings of Christ. Steve amazingly removes the notion that we need to carry anything further, as the Cross of Christ has crucified all our sufferings once and for all and by His stripes we are healed. One of the important lessons you will draw from this book, whether you are Catholic or not, is that God's healing power is personally meant for all of us, and we can all appropriate it. We can boldly come to his Throne of Grace without any doubts, make our petition known, and expect to be healed!

—MATTEO CALISI Founder and President of *The Community of Jesus*; Vatican Council member of the Pontifical Council for the Laity; Former President of the *Catholic Fraternity*

Steve Long is one of the most naturally supernatural Christians I know and his book reflects that. Steve shows that healing is accessible, available, and the Father's desire for us. He helps us to see that healing is not some mysterious roll of the dice but the intentional ongoing act of a loving Heavenly Father.

—**DAVID CAMPBELL** Regional Leader, Metropolitan Regions, *Elim Pentecostal Church*, UK

What an incredible book. As you read testimony after testimony, and scripture after scripture, you will be challenged to pray for the sick and see them healed. Pastor Steve Long shows us that anyone can pray for healing...and everyone can experience it!

—**WESLEY & STACEY CAMPBELL** Founding Pastors: *www.newlife.bc.ca;*
Founders: *www.beahero.org*

This glorious book, *My Healing Belongs to Me*, by Steve Long is a must read for those who desire to see God use them to bring healing to people in very natural and practical ways. With a wonderful combination of scripture and anecdotes, Steve nails it by powerfully revealing, God still heals today!

—**CHRIS DUPRÉ** Speaker, Worship Leader, Author of *The Wild Love of God*

As leaders we get the privilege of hearing many amazing people around the world speaking on healing the sick. All have taught us incredible truth but there are few that have inspired us by their lifestyle as much as Steve. He preaches so clearly on heaven being manifest on earth but then demonstrates it at the curry house! We warmly recommend not just his book, but the man himself!

—**STUART & CHLOE GLASSBOROW** Senior Pastors of *Catch The Fire London*

Progressive truths come when you pioneer. At one time we thought only a few prophets could prophesy. Now we know that every believer in Christ has the prophetic anointing within waiting to be activated. We may each prophecy! At one time we believed that healing belonged to only the specially gifted. Now we know that in Christ Jesus we are all specially gifted! With this view in mind, it is my honor to commend to you the teaching by Steve Long. Healing is the children's bread!

—**JAMES W. GOLL** Encounters Network; Award Winning, Best Selling Author

Steve Long is one of the most trusted pastors I know. His approach to healing is profound in its simplicity, and powerful in its impact. I'm sure you'll be challenged and encouraged as you read *My Healing Belongs to Me*.

—**BILL JOHNSON** Bethel Church, Redding, CA

I know Steve Long and deeply admire his love for God and his Word. He has written a book that reveals his passions about healing. This will encourage many people who long to be healed.

—DR. RT KENDALL Minister, *Westminster Chapel*, London (1977-2002)

I strongly endorse this book to you, it is loaded with all the scriptural references. Authority will be released into your personal witness for Jesus. You will experience his authority and power every day as I do. 13 years of ministry with power and confidence of JESUS! Why Not! You can because of what JESUS has done!

—SAM LARBIE *Right Now Jesus Centre*, London, UK

I can wholeheartedly endorse Steve's new book *My Healing Belongs to Me*. It is such a captivating personal journey of Steve's search for healing. Miracles are for today and God loves to heal people. May this book help you find the amazing love the Lord has for you.

—PASTOR IAN McCORMACK www.aglimpseofeternity.org; www.kingsgate.org.uk

With this book, Steve Long blows the lid off our limited expectations of how God can use us to release healing miracles. Using amazing testimonies of his experiences with healing, Steve makes it so easy to believe that ordinary people can live supernatural lives. Get ready to do the "greater things" that Jesus promised!

—GRANT MULLEN M.D. Author of *Emotionally Free*

At a time when the Christian church in the West is waking up once more to the supernatural dimension to our faith, it is a joy to warmly commend this book to you. A cursory review of the New Testament shows how much content the writers gave over to the healing miracles of Jesus in their testimony about him and his identity as the Messiah. How right and timely it is for us to return to this central theme and to do the works that Jesus did. Steve's approach to this topic is both biblically based and warmly pastoral. Testimony after testimony are given to show that Jesus heals today through his faithful, Spirit empowered Church. I encourage you to draw inspiration and courage from Steve's own journey into the healing ministry and 'step out of the boat' with faith declaring to a needy world: "this healing belongs to you because of what Jesus did on the cross."

—RICK OLDLAND Team Leader, *Partners in Harvest Europe*

In this book, Steve, in his characteristic style, expounds deep truths about healing the sick in a simple, easy-to-grasp way. Through faith-building stories, he takes you on his own personal journey. Definitely a must-read for those who want to embark on an adventure of doing the works of Jesus.

—SAM ONYENUFORO Senior Pastor, *Oasis Church*, Colliers Wood, England

It has been my privilege to know Steve Long for the last twenty years. I have watched both his life and his ministry develop and would go as far as to say that he is one of the most spiritual men I have had the joy of meeting. Steve is a practitioner of the healing message and I have been with him in many churches, on many occasions and seen the hand of God move very powerfully in healing through his ministry. What you have before you in this book is Steve's passion for, and journey into, a ministry that is sometimes very hard to understand. I heartily recommend this book to you and pray that you also will see more healing as you seek to serve the Lord.

—**PASTOR KEVIN PEAT** Regional Leader for *Elim Churches* in Scotland, N. Wales and N.W. England

The teaching in this book is a vital gift to the Body of Christ. At a time when many believers aren't sure if healing is for today, or have based their beliefs on what may or may not have happened to someone who needed healing, Steve takes us to the ultimate authority: God's Word.

—**BILL PRANKARD** Canadian Evangelist; President of *Bill Prankard Evangelistic Association*

This is an excellent book from a man with a true servant heart. Steve has written a very practical guide to healing, combining stories from his own first-hand experiences with clear explanation of scriptural principles. This book will enable you to apply God's healing to your own life and the lives of others.

—**NOEL RICHARDS** Worship Leader, Songwriter and Author

Twelve years ago, when I came to Canada, I started attending Catch The Fire Church. I was brokenhearted and wounded in both my body and my spirit from the torture and persecution I had received, just because I was a Christian. God used this church and Pastor Steve Long to heal my wounds and to make me whole again. This book is not just a theory or an idea, this teaching through the Holy Spirit changed and saved my life.

—**REV. MAJED EL SHAFIE** President and Founder *One Free World International for Human Rights*

I have had the privilege of joining Steve on a number of occasions where he demonstrated that healing is for everyone. All of the Body of Christ has authority to heal, and God can heal all. This book is the most practical and encouraging work I have ever read on the subject of healing. It reveals Steve's heart and struggles (that most of us go through) as he sets his spirit to work with the Holy Spirit.

—**JEREMY SINNOTT** Worship Leader and Teacher, *Catch The Fire*

Two of the many reasons I love Steve Long are his courage and transparency. He was coura-geous enough to step into some very big shoes: the senior pastor role of the church that hosted "The Toronto Blessing." His transparency is seen in this delightful book on healing, with stories of the thrill of victory and the questions left when healing didn't manifest. This book will refresh all of us on this journey of the supernatural.

—DAN SLADE International Coordinator, *Partners in Harvest*

Steve's incredible book, masterfully weaves profound biblical truth, deep theology and stun-ning real life stories of outstanding miracles that will blow your mind as you laugh and cry, supercharging you to heal the sick and receive the healing you are longing for. His depth of knowledge, conviction, simplicity, transparency and humility, irresistibly draw us to live an extraordinary life only Jesus could live through us.

—DUNCAN SMITH Co-Founder of *Catch The Fire World*; Author of *Consumed By Love*

Intrinsic truths regarding Steve's statement, "Our God is a healing God," are clearly present-ed. Issues which so often cloud our thinking regarding healing ministry are also addressed in light of scripture. Your heart will be thrilled, as was mine, journeying through the daily reality of healing ministry in the life of Jesus, echoed today in the lives of many such as Steve. This is a reality offered to us all.

—APRIL STEPHENSON Member of the *Ontario Prophetic Council*; Author of *Knowing God Through Prayer*

My Healing Belongs To Me
Published by Catch The Fire Books
272 Attwell Drive, Toronto ON M9W 6M3 Canada

Distributed worldwide by Catch The Fire Distribution. Titles may be purchased in bulk; for information, please contact distribution@catchthefire.com.

Catch The Fire ® is a registered trademark of Catch The Fire World.

ISBN 978-1-894310-61-1
Copyright © 2014 Steve Long

The Team: Emily Wright, Marcott Bernarde, Benjamin Jackson, Jonathan Puddle
Editor: Noel Gruber
Cover design: Emily Wright (Catch The Fire)
Interior layout: Marcott Bernarde (Catch The Fire)

Printed in Canada
First Edition 2014

My Healing Belongs to Me

STEVE LONG

CATCH THE FIRE
BOOKS

Foreword

Steve Long is a friend and colleague who has been a faithful co-worker for many years. He has been my right-hand in our ministry throughout the 20 plus years of the Toronto revival. I consider him and his wife Sandra to be a spiritual son and daughter to Carol and I. He has faithfully served our vision for revival and transformation for all these years. Carol and I love him and Sandra dearly.

Additionally, Steve is an able minister of the Gospel, full of the Word and full of the Spirit. It has been an absolute joy to watch Steve and Sandra learning and growing in all the values that we hold dear. A revelation of the Father's love, learning to hear His voice, healing and freedom for life's hurts and fears, and then ministering in the power of the Holy Spirit to those in need around us. Steve first received these things for himself and his family, and then began ministering in the outward journey powerfully to others.

Steve especially loves the healing ministry; bringing God's healing presence into the lives of broken hurting and ailing people, and witnessing the joyful transformation as the Holy Spirit's power breaks in upon them. And there are a number of reasons for that. He loves to see the sick healed; he loves to see the conversions that often follow; he loves to see the ongoing effect it has on families and friends, and he loves to see believers equipped to go and do likewise. What could be more satisfying to a minister of the Gospel?

In *My Healing Belongs To Me*, Steve shares how he has learned from Carol, myself and several others about healing the sick and doing miracles in the name of Jesus. In reading his book, however, I found that I learned and relearned a whole plethora of things from *him*.

Here is where he will take you: firstly, there is a great need to bring the kingdom of God not just in word only but also in power as the apostle Paul shares in first Corinthians chapter 2. Steve tells many stories about how he has done just that, in the context of his own successes, struggles and even failures. You will be brought to the place, as Steve himself was, where you know absolutely that it is your Heavenly Father's will to heal; to heal you, and then use you to bring healing to others. The transparency of his own journey will generate faith in your heart to try this, even if you stumble a few times at first while learning.

Steve gives instructions, principles, scriptures, helpful hints and stories that take you step by step through the how, why, when and where of this desperately needed ministry, and will cause you to want to 'have a go'—which is, in effect, his ultimate goal. Steve is believing God to raise up an army of ordinary Christians who nonetheless will heal the sick and demonstrate the kingdom of God everywhere they go, spreading God's love, joy and peace in so doing.

This uncomplicated yet powerful and insightful book will open the way for you to receive your own healing, and then enter into your own supernatural ministry that will bear eternal fruit for the Glory of God and the extension of His amazing and wonderful Kingdom.

Come and join Steve in high adventure! I dare you to read and then implement this book.

> *"By this is my Father glorified, that you bear much fruit; so you will be My disciples"* JOHN 15:8

John Arnott
President and Founder, Catch The Fire and Partners in Harvest
Toronto, Canada
Author of *Grace and Forgiveness* and *The Invitation*

Acknowledgements

Writing a book is like raising a child; it's hard to do alone!

I would like to acknowledge the team that helped me in the process of putting the package together. Noel Gruber, a former pastor at Catch The Fire and journalist, who took my ramblings and made them much better. Benjamin Jackson and Jonathan Puddle from Catch The Fire Books helped me with excellent advice and encouragement, guiding me through the process of becoming an author. Emily Wright and Marcott Bernarde, who designed the cover and layout: you did a marvellous job.

I would like to acknowledge Catch The Fire Toronto and the wonderful people on whom I have practised! You heard my sermons, let me pray for you and let me grow in my gifting.

I would like to acknowledge my heroes and colleagues. Roger Sapp and Bill Prankard, who taught me the basics. John and Carol Arnott, who continue to push me to attempt and believe for more. Duncan and Kate Smith, who model the bigness of God. Our Toronto and the worldwide Catch The Fire pastoral teams—you guys and gals are amazing and allow people like me to grow and mature, slowly becoming a better leader and minister of the Gospel!

I would like to acknowledge my family, who always stand behind me and think that I am the greatest (most of the time). Jon and Melissa, who encourage me to be relevant, concise, and cool. Chris and Rebekah, who ask me the tough ministry questions and who think I am cool already. My mom, in-laws, and siblings, I know what you're thinking; Steve doesn't know how to read or write! That is why I have an editor. Love you all! Dad—see you in a few years in heaven. Sandra, my amazing wife and love of my life! Always with me, always encouraging me, always loving me!

I would like to acknowledge my Father in Heaven who loves me even when I feel others don't. Jesus who saved me as a child. Holy Spirit who is with me always and is helping me become more like my Daddy and Jesus!

Table of Contents

Preface

I admit my path to a healing ministry began out of obligation. It was what people expected of a pastor and part of my responsibilities to the congregation. People needing a miracle would ask to be healed, and I was expected to pray for them. The problem was that most were not healed. As a young pastor, I prayed for years without seeing a lot of results. The experience was frustrating and humiliating for me. For the most part, I gave up on believing that God was in the healing business.

Everything changed when I came to the revival meetings at Catch The Fire Toronto. I saw healings take place all the time. I wanted to be a part of this ministry, and God made a place for me.

Several years into the revival, I heard of a healer by the name of Roger

Sapp[1]. He was speaking at a church in Newmarket, Ontario, and my wife, Sandra, and I went to see him. That's when I picked something up from him. Roger is a healing expert; he is one of the people who has had great influence in my life. In Roger, I saw myself. He is not a showman. He is not full of hype. Roger doesn't yell and scream, neither do I. He trusts the truth of the Bible as exemplified by Jesus. When he ministers, Roger simply asks people to say a powerful prayer, and many are healed on the spot.

> My healing belongs to me,
> because of what Jesus has done,
> I receive my healing now!

This little prayer has changed my life.

Bill Prankard[2] is another person that has helped me in this journey. For two years Bill and his amazing wife, Gwen, led the revival meetings at Catch The Fire Toronto. Bill is a great storyteller. He inspires people to believe in the impossible! I had the opportunity to watch Bill lead hundreds of meetings, most of them focusing on healing. He taught me how to build expectancy in people who need a healing touch. He also taught me how to interview people.

John and Carol Arnott[3], founding pastors of Catch The Fire, have been amazing mentors for me. They continue to push the boundaries and believe for more. I have been working alongside them since 1994, when the

1   Roger Sapp, *All Nations Ministries: www.allnationsmin.org* (May 30, 2014).
2   Bill Prankard, *Bill Prankard Evangelistic Association: www.bpea.com* (May 30, 2014).
3   John Arnott, *Spread the Fire Ministries: www.johnandcarol.org* (May 30, 2014)

Toronto Blessing began. They taught me how to press in and how to soak people in the anointing until their healing comes. They modeled a desire to see outstanding signs and miracles, never settling for the ordinary.

I am the result of being mentored by these great healing ministries. I've spent years watching and listening to these leaders. What I teach, how I minister, and how I lead meetings is a reflection of them. It's a bit of Roger, a bit of Bill, and lots of John and Carol. Much of what I have in this book is my take on their insights and their thoughts. I hope you hear them in what I've written.

Because of what I know from reading the Bible, combined with three decades of ministry in healing, I have something to say. My experiences range from nothing happening when I pray to seeing someone raised from the dead. I have a gift to heal the sick. I feel great injustice when I see people riding in wheelchairs, walking with limps, and battling diseases. My instinct tells me that this is not what my heavenly Father wants. The Bible confirms my beliefs.

At the beginning of this millennium, I felt the Lord asking me to write a devotional book for those who needed healing. The idea was to have a passage of Scripture tied to a short explanation, a short story, and a short prayer. My plan was to have 30 segments so people could read one per day over a month. That summer I sat on my porch most nights and came up with 30 reasons why people should be healed. I also had ideas and tools for those who were practising the ministry of healing, the result of which was another book on 30 ways to minister healing.

As I have taught on healing at our church, at conferences, at healing schools, and so on, I have had more revelation on these topics. Twice I was approached to publish my ideas and twice I felt the Lord wanted me to wait. Now it's finally time! This book is a compilation of the two devotional projects. I've expanded the ideas and updated the stories. I trust you will like the end result.

My hope is to take you on a journey of discovering how easy it is to heal people. I want to teach you and inspire you. I want to release knowledge, skills, and the faith to believe that God can use you to heal the sick! Everywhere we go, there are people who need this. I believe that it is God's will and desire that they not have pain or disease. I also believe that God uses people like you and me to be his agents for health. We don't do the actual healing, for that is the role of the Holy Spirit. Our role is simply to listen to God when he speaks to us. In the book of James, we are told to be doers of God's word. When we feel God asking us to get involved, we need to step out and act.

I believe this book will empower each of you to see God use you to bring restoration and health to your family and friends. I trust this book will also help those of you who need a healing touch.

I love seeing people healed. I know it brings a smile to God's heart. It also brings great joy to the people who need to be free from their sickness. I love being the middle man. Are you ready to begin the journey? Let's get right to it!

CHAPTER 1

My Healing Belongs to Me

When Jesus came down from the mountainside, large crowds followed him. A man with leprosy came and knelt before him and said, "Lord if you are willing, you can make me clean." Jesus reached out his hand and touched the man. "I am willing," he said. "Be clean!" Immediately he was cured of his leprosy.
MATTHEW 8:1-3

Does God want us healed?
Does God want everyone, everywhere, to be healthy all the time?

You may have asked yourself these questions, especially if you, or a loved one, is sick and in pain. You are not the first to wrestle with doubts about God's will for health and healing; for centuries, theologians and lay ministers have asked and debated the same questions. With all this discussion, you would think that the Bible is unclear on the issue. I have good news for you: the Scriptures are clear, despite the fact that the question of God's will for healing is directly referred to only in Matthew 8.

Go ahead and read through it again. When the leprous man asks, *"Lord, if you are willing,"* Jesus could have answered with a parable. He could have given a detailed reply. But Jesus' answer was concise: *"I am willing."* One question, one answer.

In my limited years of praying for the sick, I've found that one of the challenges in ministering is actually convincing people that God wants them healed. I want to convince you that God does want us healed, and that we can—and should—live without pain.

Leprosy was an incurable disease in Bible times, much like AIDS is today. Left untreated, leprosy slowly kills its victim. To this day, people with this highly infectious disease are quarantined; and yet, Jesus was not afraid of this disease. He saw it as any other sickness—an enemy of God that needed to go. Jesus touched the man, without pausing to consider that he may not be healed, and pronounced, *"Be clean!"* Can I encourage you to see the simplicity of this passage? A dying man asks a profound theological question: does God's will include healing? Jesus' response is quick and to the point: yes!

This is the only passage in all of the Bible where this question is asked and thus the only place where the answer is given. God is willing to heal. Not only is God willing to heal, but it would appear that he wants to heal men and women of every kind of sickness — whether the root cause is an accident, demonic influence, generational curse, or sin.

Whether you are in a little or a lot of pain.
Whether there is a name for your disease or not.
Whether the doctors say it can or can't be treated.
God's will is simple, straightforward, and obvious: *"I am willing!"*

MINISTERING TO MY FIRST LEPER

My first trip to visit Rolland and Heidi Baker at Iris Ministries was in 1999, before they became famous. They had only two churches, one at the orphanage, and the other at a dump. My first day in Maputo, Mozambique, involved a leper.

Our team had joined an outreach in the inner city, near a market. It was dark and most streetlights were out. Heidi asked me to do a short healing talk so I spoke on Matthew 8 and shared about the leper. Unbeknownst to me, there was a leper at the meeting. When I finished my talk, and our team started ministering, this man came to me assuming I knew how to heal lepers. I didn't understand him and he didn't understand me, so he took my hand and put it on his leg. Big mistake! My hand touched rotting flesh and bone. My first thought was *why didn't I talk about headaches?* My faith was not very high. I was overwhelmed by the reality of what my hand was touching. I prayed for the man, but nothing happened.

As I thought about it afterwards and pondered how Jesus had intentionally touched the leprous man, I realized that I had a long way to go in being like him. Jesus, knowing all the implications of touching a leper, did it without even thinking. He knew that his Father wanted all lepers healed. This picture of Jesus demonstrates what the heart of our Father has always been.

Numbers 23:19 says,

> *God is not a man, that he should lie;*
> *not a human being, that he should change his mind.*
> *Does he speak and then not act?*
> *Does he promise and not fulfill?*

Likewise, Hebrews 13:8 states, *"Jesus Christ is the same yesterday and today and forever."* The immutability of God is a fancy way of saying that God does not change. Not only does he stay the same, but he is actually incapable of changing. God can't lie. He can't change his mind or break a promise. If God doesn't change, then everything in the Bible relating to healing—the promises of God in the Old Testament, the words of Jesus in the New Testament, and the teachings of the apostles — is valid today.

There is a teaching in many churches called dispensationalism. Simply put, it states that God works differently with humanity in different eras of human history. So in the era when Jesus lived, he and his followers were used by God to heal. But, now that the New Testament era is ended, God operates differently. I believe that the purpose behind this man-made doctrine, which in my opinion does not have any sound biblical support, was developed as an explanation for the times that people are not healed.

Scholar B.B. Warfield (1851–1921)[4] is an example of this. His wife was hit by lightning early in their marriage and was paralyzed for the rest of her life. Warfield is said to have earnestly sought reasons from the Lord as to why some people, including his wife, where not healed. The best he could come up with was that in these last days God has stopped healing. God used to heal when Jesus was on earth. He was into healing when the apostles lived, but when they died God changed and stopped healing people.

The only problem with this well-meaning teaching is that it goes against the clear teaching of God's Word from Hebrews 13:8. If God wanted to heal then, he must still want to heal. This is wonderful news for us. It's another reason that we can believe God's will today is to heal us!

This simple verse was the passage that God used to provoke me to think outside the theological box in which I was raised and trained. I had a deep conviction that God's Word was absolutely true, yet this verse kept nagging at me. If you've grown up in a culture that believes that miracles and healings don't happen, circular thinking can settle in your mind. Because we don't believe they will happen, we don't pray in faith or expect anything. Because we don't push in, many of our friends and family don't receive their healing. Our negative experience has just proved our belief that healing isn't for today.

Over a period of time I began to see passages come alive, such as James 5 where we are commanded to pray for the sick. Why would James give clear teaching on how to minister healing to people if that was only going to be

---

4   Benjamin Breckinridge Warfield, *Counterfeit Miracles* (New York: Charles Scribner's Sons, 1918).

an option for another fifteen to twenty years? It must mean that healing is available for now, especially since God doesn't change.

WALTER'S STORY

I remember the first major healing meeting that we had at our Baptist church in Mississauga, Ontario. John and Anne Freel were the pastors and Sandra and I served as the associate pastors. One of the deacons, Walter, was scheduled for back surgery on a Monday. He asked if we would anoint him with oil as per James 5. We agreed, but decided we would do it at the Sunday night meeting. Sunday nights in our church meant a younger crowd who were more open to us doing things differently.

John poured oil on Walter, prayed over him, and that was that. We didn't ask him how his back felt; we didn't know to do that. Walter went to the hospital the next day as planned and came home early — there was no need for an operation. We couldn't believe it! Our prayers and some extra virgin cooking oil had healed Walter. From that day on, we ministered healing to everyone who asked. We began to see more extraordinary healings. By pressing in, we ourselves had proved that God doesn't change. God's heart is still for those who are in pain and who have sickness. Glory to God!

GOD STILL OPPOSES EVERY WORK OF SATAN

As thrilled as we were for Walter, it should have been no surprise to us that God wanted to oppose what Satan was trying to do to him. Of course God wanted Walter healed. How could we think differently in light of verses such as John 10:10: *"The thief comes only to steal and kill and destroy; I have come that they may have life, and have it to the full."*

This passage is one of the clearest teachings of Jesus on what God wants. Satan wants to steal everything you have, including your health. Satan wants to kill you. One of his tactics is to hinder you through sickness, disease, and accidents. Satan is out to destroy us, especially those of us who follow Jesus. Satan is opposed to everything God stands for.

Jesus, on the other hand, spoke clearly about what he stood for and why he came to this world: *"I have come that they may have life, and have it to the full."* Let me put that phrase into today's terms: Jesus came to give us the absolute best — the most rewarding and satisfying life we could ever dream of having! This includes good health. No one would say that a life full of sickness and suffering is a good or full life. As Jesus reveals the reason for being sent to earth, he is also making a statement about the Father's desire for us to be healthy.

When the apostle John writes a greeting to the church in 3 John 1:2, he says, *"Dear friend, I pray that you may enjoy good health and that all may go well with you, even as your soul is getting along well."* God's desire is always good health.

WHY SICKNESS?

Despite what I believe, I'm not so naïve as to assume that everyone lives in perfect health all the time, but I can tell you why some don't: Satan is still opposed to God's plan and is constantly at work against us.

The question then arises, is God asleep at the steering wheel? Did God set things in motion and then go on a prolonged vacation? No, no, no! God is active in our lives, which is why he sent the Holy Spirit to be with us forever. God, through the Holy Spirit, fights on our behalf against every attempt that Satan brings to steal, kill, and destroy. It is a daily battle that often takes place behind the scenes without our awareness. Paul wrote in Ephesians 6:12: *"For our struggle is not against flesh and blood but against the rulers, against the authorities, against the powers of this dark world and against the spiritual forces of evil in the heavenly realms."* He knew that there is an unseen battle where the Holy Spirit, allied with angels, fights against Satan and his demonic beings.

Paul and Peter blamed Satan for sickness. Paul admonishes us in Ephesians 6:13: *"Therefore put on the full armor of God, so that when the day of evil comes you may be able to stand your ground."* He knew that God is still in the healing and restoration business. Peter says the same thing when he briefs Cornelius and his friends about the ministry of Jesus. In Acts 10:38, he speaks of *"how he went around doing good and healing all who were under the power of the devil, because God was with him."* Peter clearly blames Satan for bringing sickness and credits Jesus with counteracting it. This is one of the foundational passages of Scripture for me when it comes to knowing the will of God. Simply put, if Satan is active in bringing sickness to your body, then that means that God is active in healing you.

When there was a showdown between Elijah and the prophets of Baal,

Elijah taunted the false prophets that their gods must be asleep, as they were not helping them. You'll remember that fire from heaven came instantaneously onto the sacrifice when Elijah called out to God. God is alive and desires to be very active in our lives, if we will let him.

You may be asking the obvious question: Why haven't I been healed? The quick answer is that Satan has had access to your life in some way. Satan takes every opportunity to steal our healing. Our sin, curses from others, our negative responses to the hurts of others, they all open the door for disease to come our way. In order to receive breakthrough, we need to appropriate the healing that God has for us. I remember once seeing a list of about 40 reasons why people are not healed. The list was very shocking, in that a bunch of the topics were issues that I had.

HEALING ON A PLANE

Several years ago John and Carol led a team of about fifteen to Africa to visit a healing specialist. It was very different and provoked as many questions as there were answers. Just hours before we left, the pastor prayed an impartation prayer for each of us.

We left on a British Airways plane, which was almost empty. I moved ahead of our group and grabbed four seats in the middle. As we were moving towards the runway, a British man across from me began to choke and gasp for air. He quickly turned blue. It was obvious that something wasn't right. John Arnott and I both jumped out of our seats to assist the man.

Because I was closer, I got there first. As flight attendants saw the situation they ran to his aid as well. But before they got to him, I did something with my new impartation. I went into the seat behind him thinking that I would do the Heimlich manoeuvre. I told the man that I was a pastor and was going to pray for him. He nodded and choked in response. I took it as consent.

As soon as I put my hand on his back, he threw up violently. I'm talking 3 meters (10 feet) of spew, which went over all the seats in front of him. It was a good thing that they were empty!

By now the flight attendants had arrived and the first one there heard me say that I was going to pray. He clearly made the connection between what happened and my prayer as he let me be in charge. I told everyone that he was going to be fine.

The head flight attendant came to us from business class. She wanted to turn back to the airport to have the man seek medical attention. For some reason I said it wasn't necessary and the younger flight attendant agreed with me. He said that I knew what I was doing. (Not sure that this was true, I was just flowing in the anointing at short notice.) They cleaned up the man and the seating area, moved him to business class, and we took off to London, England. After we were in the air I went to the front of the plane to talk to the man. It turned out he was in the country for business. He wasn't a follower of Jesus and didn't have any interest in becoming one.

John Arnott later told me that his discernment was telling him that this man had slept with a local woman and may have picked up a demonic spirit or curse to kill him. If that was true, one would think he would be open to learning a lesson after almost dying on the plane. Our choices can open up the door to sickness, but God is always ready to help us close the door and get our healing.

WHY DIDN'T JESUS PRAY?

Sometimes what is not said is as important as what is. There is another truth that we can pull from the leprosy healing in Matthew: Jesus never prayed before ministering healing to someone. I dare you to take a look at all the gospel accounts and find one place where Jesus asked God what he should do for someone's healing. You won't find it! He didn't ever stop to ask God if he should minister. There is a wonderful truth behind this absence of prayer: Jesus did not pray because he already knew what his Father wanted! He knew that his Father wanted people well and so he didn't need to ask, not even once.

The only other explanation we could give is that Jesus was arrogant, seeking to gain attention for himself, and couldn't care less what his Father wanted. I think we all know that this isn't even close to the truth.

When we pray to God, one of the reasons we pray is that we are unsure of what he wants. Many of our prayers sound something like this: "God I don't know what is going on here, but you do. Can you please help?" There is nothing wrong with this prayer, but it demonstrates that we don't know what God's will is in that situation. When we know what God wants, it affects how we communicate with him. We have every right to say to God, "Your Word says that you will heal my friend, and so do it." Would you agree that this prayer is bolder than the previous one? The second prayer communicates confidence in what God desires. We know what he has already said on the subject and we are holding him to it. Jesus already knew what his Father wanted when it came to healing the various diseases that he encountered. He knew that God wanted everyone to be healed—no exceptions!

You will not find one instance in the Gospels of Jesus turning someone away who wanted ministry for healing. Every person who came to Jesus was healed regardless of his or her disease. The history of their suffering was irrelevant. No need to ask for God's permission. He knew that God wanted people well.

If you lived in Bible times, Jesus would have done for you what he did for everyone else. He would have ministered to you and you would have been healed. Today Jesus is seated beside the Father, constantly interceding for us and bringing our needs before him. This is great news!

KNOWING GOD'S WILL

One of the times I was in Curitiba, Brazil, I saw a young lady in a wheelchair while we were worshiping. When it was my turn to preach, I began by leading a healing segment. Something inside me drew me to this woman. I didn't pray and ask God who to minister to. I just knew.

She was 22 years old and was paralyzed from the armpits down as a result of a car accident. As I ministered to her the Holy Spirit began to be evidenced in her body. She was able to feel heat in her legs and torso for the first time in seven years!

Without knowing her, her situation, or her faith level, I knew that God wanted to do a miracle in her body. Just like Jesus, there was no reason to wait until I had a go-ahead from God. I knew what he wanted to do in her life.

These words of knowledge are wonderful tools for us in ministry. I get these random thoughts a lot. I have learned that when a thought comes into my mind from out of the blue, God is speaking to me and I need to respond as quickly as possible. Restaurants are the primary place I do ministry, as the people I work with at our church are all followers of Jesus. I love to tune in to the flow of God's thoughts when I am out of our building.

On my first trip to Brazil, I was taken with other pastors for lunch after a meeting. There were about twelve of us, and I was seated by my translator, Sergio. During the meal I had a random thought that the lady who was serving us was in pain. So the next time she came over to our table I had Sergio ask her for me. I wasn't prepared for her response, but God was. I had been set up on this one. She stared at me as if I was a ghost. She proceeded to tell us that she had a degenerating bone disease that causes severe pain. Just that morning, she had asked God to show her he was real by sending someone to relieve her pain, now here I was asking about it.

It turns out she was the owner of restaurant. We went to a room off to the side and I had her say a simple prayer:

My healing belongs to me
because of what Jesus has done
I receive my healing now!

She was instantly healed! All the pain that was in every bone in her body left in an instant. She cried and cried. I led her to the Lord. Her young daughter was standing beside her and we found out that she had the same problem, only worse. The little girl, perhaps thirteen or fourteen years old, was wearing a plastic body suit to keep her straight. She said the prayer and was also healed. More crying!

The woman then asked what I could do for her son. She said he was the worst of them; his bones had been broken 24 times to help to relieve the pain. Because he was at school, we said the prayer for his healing in faith before leaving the restaurant. Two nights later, the whole family came to the last of our meetings in their city and sat in the front row. The mom hugged me and told me that her son had come home from school without pain. All of them had been completely pain-free for two days. Not only that, but the little girl had grown two inches. I started the meeting by having them share their story and gave an opportunity to people who wanted receive Jesus. The husband and son were first to respond to the invitation.

How did this healing happen? I had a word of knowledge (a God-thought) and acted on it. God wanted to answer the woman's prayer and I was perhaps the only believer she would meet that day. God spoke to me to help me to know his will.

THE DAILY ROUTINE OF JESUS

Just as what Jesus didn't do gives us insight into the heart of God, what he *did* do communicates the same truth. His daily routine gives us a glimpse into the will of God concerning healing. In Acts 10:38 it says that Jesus *"went around doing good and healing all."* Healing was a regular occurrence. It was always happening in the ministry of Jesus. The primary purpose of Jesus coming to earth was to die on the cross for our sins, but he accomplished so much more.

In studying the New Testament, it would appear that 20 per cent of the accounts of Jesus are stories of healing. There are 41 different healing stories, and 727 out of 3779 verses in the Gospels relate to healing. Luke alone has eighteen stories of Jesus healing the sick.

I'm not sure how many hours Jesus worked in an average day. What I do know is that those living in developing nations today work anywhere from twelve- to sixteen-hour days, seven days a week. Let's say that Jesus had a ten-hour workday. If the Scriptures are anywhere close in showing how Jesus spent his time, that would mean that Jesus spent two hours each day ministering healing to men and women. One-fifth of his time he spent leading healing meetings. That adds up to thousands of hours of healing during the three-and-a-half years he was in ministry.

If God did not want us healed why would he have had Jesus spend that much time in a healing ministry? Seven times in the book of John, Jesus said that he didn't do anything by himself. He only did what the Father wanted. To ask his Son to spend that much time each day ministering healing tells me that God's will is for our healing. As we read the Scriptures, such as Matthew 8 and 9, we see passage after passage of Jesus healing. One would almost think that this was the primary reason Jesus came to earth.

God is not only a healing God, but his heart is that we walk in that under-standing. He wants us to be confident in his desire to mend our bodies and that he has power to do so.

God's desire is to minister to you today through the person of the Holy Spirit. Jesus was God's representative on earth. He promised that when he left he would send someone else to take over his ministry. The Holy Spirit is that person, and he can minister to you today.

SET UP ONCE AGAIN

I need to constantly remind myself that Jesus ministered healing every day. So, I should be aware that opportunities to minister will come to me each day as well. One particular day, as I sat on my front porch writing, a post office van pulled up in front of my neighbour's home and the mailman got out to deliver mail to our street. I looked up as the car parked and heard the Holy Spirit say, *He has pain.*

As he walked to my neighbor's house he said to me, "How are you feeling?" Not "How are you doing?" which is a more normal greeting. He initiated a conversation about health. I told him I was doing well. As I responded to what I already knew, that he was in pain, I heard the Lord give me specific information.

"How are your knees?" I asked.

Well, wouldn't you know, he had a rare type of arthritis. I asked him if he would like the pain to stop. He looked at me and began to tell me of his special diet. I clarified and asked if he want the pain to go right away. Now I had his attention.

I explained that I was writing a book on healing; if he had ten seconds we could say a prayer. He told me he was Catholic and said prayers all the time, so he repeated this after me:

> My healing belongs to me,
> because of what Jesus has done.
> I receive my healing, now.

Nothing seemed to change, and he thanked me for praying for him. Two days later I saw him again; his knee had improved and he thanked me again for praying for him.

I love the fact that God is active in the healing business. He not only gives us opportunities to go to people, but he actively brings people to us!

SUPERNATURAL GIFTS

None of the stories I've shared so far would have been possible without the Holy Spirit and the supernatural anointing of his gifts. God not only modelled his heart in healing us, but also sent Holy Spirit and released supernatural gifts to enable us to do the same. Consider 1 Corinthians 12:7-11:

> Now to each one the manifestation of the Spirit is given for the common good.
> To one there is given through the Spirit the message of wisdom, to another the

message of knowledge by means of the same Spirit, to another faith by the same Spirit, to another gifts of healing by that one Spirit, to another miraculous powers, to another prophecy, to another distinguishing between spirits, to another speaking in different kinds of tongues, and to still another the interpretation of tongues. All these are the work of one and the same Spirit, and he gives them to each one, just as he determines.

Spiritual gifts are given to each person when they become a follower of Jesus. The gifts, which are also referenced in Romans 12, Ephesians 4, and 1 Peter 4, cover a wide range of special anointed abilities, but fall into three general categories: speaking gifts, serving gifts, and ministry gifts.

While the gifts cover a multitude of possible ministry areas, I'd like to focus specifically on physical healing. If each of the gifts is given for the common good, what is the common good that comes from healing gifts? Simply put, it's to help sick people become well. Not only is there a specific healing gift (or gifts), but several of the others can also be directly used in a healing ministry: The supernatural word of wisdom can be used to know what to do for a sick person. The supernatural word of knowledge helps us to identify specific disease or to get clarity on an issue, person or problem. Discerning of spirits can help identify the source of the illness. The gift of faith helps the person ministering healing to have confidence and minister with boldness. The performing of miracles allows for spectacular healings that would not happen naturally over time. The gift of tongues let us minister spirit-to-spirit and bypass any mental blocks that stop the healing.

It would seem to me that physical healing is perhaps *the* primary reason for gifts to be given, since so many of them can be used in healing. What's more, when the healing gift is mentioned, it is the only word that is used consistently in plural form. I'm convinced that this is because God wants many different expressions of how we partner with Holy Spirit to bring about healing. God wants people healed so much that he has given his people multiple avenues to team up with him to that end. It is almost as if God so desperately wants us to be healed that he has purposely down-loaded many healing options to us. It is as if he is saying we shouldn't have any problems with healing every person who comes our way. He has made it simple for us to minister healing and made it easy for us to be healed.

In 1995, we made healing the focus of our Sunday night meetings at Catch The Fire. Hundreds came every Sunday and often hundreds were healed. We have seen a large variety of guest speakers who flow in healing gifts. I've seen people minister healing exclusively through words of knowledge. I've seen some people minister healing through faith, and others through discerning of spirits. There is no single formula.

PARALYZED ARM HEALED

I was speaking recently to a small group of people who attend an African and a Brazilian church. The two congregations share the same building and occasionally do meetings together. I spoke on a Saturday night at an announced healing meeting.

The first man to be healed responded by coming to the front of the room while I was still speaking. I hadn't got to the end of my talk, but he was already convinced. He was about 60 years old, spoke Portuguese, and had a significant need. Sometimes I ask people ahead of time what their problem is, but this time I didn't. I simply placed my hand on him while I kept talking. I explained that by attending the meeting he showed enough faith to be healed. Why come to a healing meeting if you don't think it will happen? Together we said my simple healing prayer:

> My healing belongs to me,
> because of what Jesus has done.
> I receive my healing now!

Emotions quickly stirred in him. I didn't know what his physical problem was. As I touched him, he began to sob deeply. Everyone stopped what they were doing and looked at the man.

There were about 50 people in the meeting, and most of us were at the front and near to him. Through tears he told us that his hand was now awake. It turned out that his arm had been paralyzed. I didn't get the full story, but my guess is that he'd had a stroke. He sobbed in the arms of the other man. How did this man get his healing?

Because of the supernatural power of God.
Because he exhibited faith.
Because a friend cared and stood with him in agreement.
Because a person flowed in the gifts of the Spirit.
Because God wants everyone, everywhere, healed!

If you've been struggling to believe God's will is to heal you, I want to encourage you to read on and allow the truth of God's heart to saturate your mind, body, and spirit. Don't allow Satan to steal from you what God wants to give you. Agree with me right now, wherever you are, that God wants healing for you, your family, and your friends.

Would you pray this prayer with me?

> *Father, forgive me for questioning your motives and your desires for my friends, my family, and me. Please begin to erase every lie that I have accepted into my spirit relating to healing. Eradicate every untruth relating to my sickness and pain. I choose today to believe what your Bible says; you are willing to heal me. I accept my healing now based on the unchangeable Word of God. Please come and touch my body and take away every bit of pain, because your will and desire is for me to be healed. In the name of Jesus, amen!*

Now let me pray for you:

> *Father I pray in the name of Jesus for my friend. I command healing to come into their body wherever there is sickness or disease. Father, come and oppose every evil strategy that Satan has already achieved in my friend's life, and every plan that he is making against them. I welcome the Holy Spirit to bring peace where there is pain. I welcome you God to come and rid them of every trace of sickness. I speak health into your physical body: wherever there is pain, it goes to the cross. Jesus died on the cross to provide your healing and to seal the fate of Satan. I speak to your sickness and tell it to go. I command every demonic activity in your body to stop and be reversed. I welcome the*

wonderful peace that comes from our Father to come into your body right now in the name of Jesus! Father, I partner with you for the good of my friend. Heal them in the name of Jesus, amen.

CHAPTER 2

Sources of Healing Power

Do you remember Waldo? Waldo was an interesting looking character in children's books who was hidden in a crowded picture for readers to find. Sounds easy, but it wasn't. Where does healing comes from? Just like Waldo, the answer it a lot deeper than it might seem at first glance. This chapter is all about looking at the source of our healing in order to allow us to receive what is rightfully ours.

Matthew 8 provides one of the best segments in the four-gospel account of Jesus' life regarding healing. After four simple stories of Jesus healing a leper, a lame boy, a mother-in-law, and an entire crowd, Matthew interjects an editorial comment. Matthew, you may remember, did not write his account in a chronological format. While it generally follows the events of Jesus' life, Matthew arranges segments to allow for certain themes to develop for the reader. His stories are pieced together to allow him to give a topical overview of the life of Jesus. So the four healing stories in Matthew 8 may not have all happened back-to-back as he records them, but he has written them together for a purpose. Matthew knows where he is going with his narrative and that his conclusion will be that each of these stories tells us where our healing comes from. Let's explore these together.

The first story (Matthew 8:1-4) relates to the will of God. Does God want people healed? Yes. The second story (Matthew 8:5-13) provides a glimpse into how Jesus did ministry. The centurion, a man in authority, figured out that Jesus was a middleman acting on behalf of a higher commander. The third story (Matthew 8:14-15) happens during lunch on a Sabbath day at Peter's home. It illustrates that Jesus simply responded to people in need. He always met needs. The fourth story (Matthew 8:16) is about what happened later that same day, when those in a large crowd were all healed. The fact that the crowd was all healed demonstrates two things: one of them is that there are no reasons or excuses that limit healing. The second is that there is no limit to what the anointing can do!

Now Matthew gets to his point in verse 17: "*This was to fulfill what was spoken through the prophet Isaiah: 'He took up our infirmities and bore our diseases.'*" He sums up the four stories by saying that Jesus healed people to fulfill a prophetic statement from Isaiah 53.

JESUS' TORTURE, OUR HEALING

If you saw *The Passion of the Christ*, you will have experienced a measure of how Jesus was horrifically tortured. Isaiah 53:4 told us this would happen. The prophet Isaiah, speaking 800 years before the event, said that healing was going to be accessible. The four stories that Matthew tells were possible because of what took place during the Passion of Jesus.

Let me clear up a point that many miss. What happened on the cross when Jesus died? The penalty of our sins was dealt with. Forgiveness of our sins became possible. If that is the case, why then did the Passion have to be so horrendous? Why did Jesus have to suffer so much before his death? Matthew 8:17 answers that. Jesus suffered so that we don't have to. While his death brought us salvation from our sins, his suffering brings life to our bodies. The more he suffered, the less we need to remain in our illnesses. The weight of your sickness and pain was combined with that of mine and the rest of mankind and placed on Jesus' shoulders.

Matthew sums up Isaiah 53:5 by saying, *"and by his wounds we are healed."* Healing happens because Jesus has already paid the price. His Passion, the beating and whipping, means that healing is accessible to everyone, everywhere, all the time. Now we need to appropriate what is rightfully ours.

GLASS-EYE HEALING

I was at a great Holy Spirit, Baptist Church in Campinas, Brazil, which is led by Pastor Edino Melo. The church had just finished a forty-day fast in preparation for a special offering to build their new building. It was a Monday, and I was scheduled as the guest speaker. There was obviously a lot of excitement in anticipation of the announcement of the total amount. I don't think anyone was there for me, they were there to give sacrificially.

Several other pastors and leaders were there, and Pastor Edino asked me and the other guests if we would bless each person as they gave their gift. So people lined up in four lines to both give money and receive prayer.

If you know Brazil, you know that people were not anticipating a simple blessing prayer; they were wanting healing, deliverance, prayers for family, prayers for jobs, prayers for marriage partners, etc. This took quite a while. I was given a member of the congregation to act as my translator. It turns out that he was a very wealthy businessman who had just joined the church two weeks ago after giving his life to Jesus. At the end of the offering time, my translator asked me if I could pray for his eyes. He told me that he had a glass eye. His doctors had removed his pupil three years before, after an accident. His glass eye couldn't produce tears and made his eye socket sore. I prayed, but nothing seemed to happen.

After I preached, Pastor Melo came up and announced the offering total. It was almost double what they needed to start the building and just slightly shy of what they needed to complete it. They were hoping to have a two-stage build, now they could go for the whole thing at once. The excitement was awesome! We finished off the night with prayer and ministry.

It was after midnight when we finally left the hall. In Brazil, it is never too late to eat meat, so off we went to a home for our evening meal. The businessman and his wife were invited as well. As we ate, all of us pastors exchanged our healing stories. Suddenly my translator jumped in to the conversation and said that his eye felt better. What? We all looked at him, including his wife. He told us that all the soreness in his eye was gone and that during the celebration regarding the offering, he cried!

How does this kind of thing happen? It is because Jesus has already paid for your healing and mine. Miracles can happen because of what happened to Jesus. I have a theory regarding the beating of Jesus. I can't prove it, but when you get to heaven you will find out if I'm right. I believe that every part of Jesus' body was damaged while he was being flogged and beaten. I believe that as Jesus was having his flesh torn off, his organs were exposed. I believe that the whips hit his eyes, his ears, his arms, legs, etc. With each mark on his body I believe our healing was sealed for that part of our bodies. Let's thank Jesus for suffering for us, allowing us to receive healing and to be used by his Spirit to bring healing to others.

Jesus, thank you so much for dying for us. Thank you for the hours you spent being tortured on our behalf. Thank you for embracing the cross as you headed to Golgotha. Thank you for enduring the pain of the whippings and the anguish of the nails as they went into your hands and feet. Thank you for accepting the torture that came with dying on a cross. Thank you for paying this ultimate price for us. Jesus, you did not deserve any of this but we are so grateful that you traded places with us! Thank you for not only dying so that our sins could be forgiven, but also for bringing us to the place where our infirmities and our diseases have already been carried away. We bless you Jesus for this incredible sacrifice. Thank you for your gift to us today. Amen.

THE KINGDOM OF GOD

Most of the healings that we see in the life of Jesus were instantaneous. With just a few exceptions, when Jesus ministered, people were healed.

Obviously he had not been beaten or died yet, so how were the healings possible? This is where the *Where's Waldo* depth comes in. Jesus' torture is but one piece of the healing puzzle. The next piece is simple: healing is part of the kingdom of God.

In Matthew 4:23-24 we read:

Jesus went throughout Galilee, teaching in their synagogues, preaching the good news of the kingdom, and healing every disease and sickness among the people. News about him spread all over Syria, and people brought to him all who were ill with various diseases, those suffering severe pain, the demon-possessed, those having seizures, and the paralyzed, and he healed them.

When Jesus began his ministry, he was a trendsetter. He set the pace and led by example in everything he did. In one sense, all of history was leading up to him. Once Jesus arrived we transitioned to new rules, kingdom rules! He talked about the kingdom constantly: *"I must proclaim the good news of the kingdom of God to the other towns also, because that is why I was sent"* (Luke 4:43).

When the followers of Jesus began their ministry, they also picked up on the kingdom theme. I find it fascinating that John, Paul, and others who were preachers, all followed suit and talked about the kingdom of God. It is one of the primary themes of the New Testament. Philip *"preached the good news of the kingdom of God and the name of Jesus Christ"* (Acts 8:12).

We see in Acts 19:8 that Paul did the same. *"He entered the synagogue and spoke boldly there for three months, arguing persuasively about the kingdom of God."*

What was the kingdom message Jesus preached? It was that the kingdom of God had arrived. He gave evidence that a new day had come by doing things that had rarely been done before, namely *"healing every disease and sickness among the people"* (Matthew 4:23). Much has been written about the kingdom of God and it is not my intention to provide a full theological exposition. I love simplicity, and as I'm sure you've noticed, I love to get to the bottom line as quick as I can. So here it goes: the kingdom is all about Jesus establishing a new way of living. Or perhaps better stated, the kingdom is the way that God has always wanted things to be.

Before Jesus came, we didn't know how to get connected to this mystical, far-off kingdom. Jesus modeled what the new kingdom was all about. He preached about it in sermons such as his lengthy talk on a mountain (Matthew 5-7), where he laid out what the values of the kingdom are and how we attain them.

One of the kingdom values is that God wants people to live in victory. If Jesus is the King who won the battle, then we all get to share in his victory. A major benefit of his victory through the cross is that sickness, disease, pain, and any kind of ailment are now optional. There is no need for people to remain sick. As I said, Jesus has already paid the price to set us free from infirmities and disease. If we want to appropriate healing, it is there for us.

The kingdom message can be summed up in what we know as the Lord's

Prayer. Jesus begins his model prayer by focusing on our wonderful Father, then he switches to talk about the kingdom. *"Your kingdom come, your will be done, on earth as it is in heaven"* (Matthew 6:10). This is a command! The prayer communicates that everything happening in heaven is supposed to be happening on earth. This is our Father's will and this is what the kingdom is all about. In heaven there is no poverty. In heaven there are no bad relationships. In heaven there is no sickness or disease. That is our Father's will and what he wants on earth!

When Jesus brought the kingdom, every person who requested ministry was healed. Whole crowds were healed in one sitting, with no exceptions. One of the reasons healing was so easy for Jesus, and why it is supposed to be easy for us today, is that healing is part of the package that came when Jesus established his kingdom. When Jesus announced the kingdom, he linked healing to it. Healing still comes today because it is a part of the kingdom package. Jesus lived a hundred per cent of the time within the kingdom. So can we!

THE KINGDOM IS HERE, BUT STILL TO COME

But we still have a way to go. John Wimber, founder of the Vineyard group of churches, used to say that the kingdom has come and is coming. What he meant is that we are in the kingdom, but we haven't entered into its fullness.

On June 1944, the Allied Nations landed at Normandy to begin the liberation of Europe. Eventually the war was won; all the Axis Powers surrendered, and France, Germany, Poland, and many other nations began to set up their "kingdoms" anew. Did it take time? Yes. Were there hiccups?

Definitely. Were any of these nations fully functional right away? No. The D-Day invasions were a success, and many other battles were won, but the process of living by new rules took much longer. Germany remained divided for 45 years!

It's the same with the kingdom of God. Jesus won the battle; however, Satan still has his terrorist tactics that scare many people into believing that the war is still on. It's not.

So here we are living in victory, yet knowing that there is still more to come. We see lots of evidence that New Testament principles work and we should continue to expect them to. The kingdom was ushered in by Jesus and continues to be released among us.

MOTHER DIAGNOSED WITH CANCER

Many years ago one of the ladies from Catch The Fire Toronto was diagnosed with cancer. She was married with two children in their teen years. Sandra and I went to their home to pray. We prayed that she would be healed, that she would be free of cancer and pain. I don't know why, but the Lord only answered one of our prayers.

The lady began to fade in strength as the cancer became more aggressive. Sadly, she died from this horrific disease. The one prayer of ours that was answered was regarding pain. To the day she died she never took a painkiller, not one. At her funeral this was one of the topics addressed from her life. Her husband thanked the Lord for the grace that his wife was given. Her nurses shared that this was highly unusual and that her faith had to be the reason. God was glorified despite the fact that she passed away prematurely.

No one on earth has all the answers or revelation as to why some of our prayers go unanswered. But this is what I do know: healing has been provided for us because the kingdom is here. And yet the kingdom is still being unfolded, which means that there will be a better understanding in the future.

THE COMPASSION OF GOD

He sent forth his word and healed them; he rescued them from the grave. Let them give thanks to the Lord for his unfailing love and his wonderful deeds for men. PSALM 107:20-21

The psalmist links healing to the unfailing love that God has for us. At the very centre of healing is the compassionate heart of God. John tells us that *"God is love"* (1 John 4:8), and he goes on to say that *"He first loved us"* (1 John 4:19). Every aspect of what God does flows through his attribute of love. It is impossible for God not to screen every thought, every action, every directive, and every response through the incredible compassion that he has for us. God's love is unending; it has no limits. He cannot help but love us despite what our past is, where we are now, and what our future holds. God is love right through to his very core.

As we've looked at the source of healing, it is obvious that healing originates with the Father. James 1:17 says that *"every good and perfect gift comes from the Father of lights."* The healing and mending of our bodies comes from him.

Why is it that God heals people?
Why is it that he had Jesus represent him day after day in a healing ministry?
Why is it that he inspires James to teach us how to minister to the sick?
Why are there hundreds of stories in the Bible of people who received their healing?

It is because God loves mankind. John 3:16, probably the most famous verse in the Bible, begins with *"for God so loved the world."* Because of God's love, his never-ending concern for our well being, he gave Jesus to us. To this day, God continues to share his love with us. Healing is a way for God to express his love. He cannot help but always think of what is best for us. Time after time, his love compels him to act—and healing is one of those actions.

Because Jesus always represented the Father, he was also driven by this love. Many times Jesus' heart went out to a sick person he met. It's as if when he saw a person in pain, sick, or demonized, he had no choice but to act.

FAMILY CAMP IN CARLISLE

I was once at a family camp in Carlisle, in the north of England, ministering for a great church in Wrexham, Wales, with leaders Nick and Sue Pengelly.

We had several healing opportunities in the meeting and most people were healed as they ministered to each other. One of the men that I was asked to minister to was named John and was in his forties.

At the age of one, John developed a cancer that was somehow connected to his eyes. His doctor's only option was to remove both his eyes to stop the spread of cancer. It was amazing to feel the compassion that quickly moved my heart as I heard John's story. Everything in me was desperate to see new eyes for this man. Many folks came and stood with their friend once they realized that I was taking a prolonged time to minister to him. Several men had tears in their eyes as we prayed for about 45 minutes.

Why were they moved to tears? Because of their love for John and their knowing that losing his eyes at such a young age was not what God had intended. At one point as I was ministering, we asked God to give John a picture of what it was like before he lost his eyes. With his spiritual vision, John saw himself. When he saw also Jesus, he broke down crying. He had not seen Jesus with him before. He hadn't thought of asking the Lord to reveal where he was prior to the surgery.

Why was Jesus with John as a one-year-old baby with cancer? Because of the compassionate love of Father God!

As I've guided people to look in the Spirit about key times in their past, almost everyone is filled with tears as they see Jesus and his compassion for them. His promise is to always be with us, yet we seldom stop to look to see where he is in times of stress and turmoil. God is with us at all times. His love allows healing to be available for the taking. A simple touch by

Jesus instantly brings healing. A God-word from any of us removes pain. A prayer releases life into a sick body.

As you minister to people, remember to feel the love that God has for the sick. Remind yourself to tap into the love that God has for those with pain. Feel his compassion for people's struggles. I've found that many times, as I have been drawn into the affection of his heart for someone, it has been easier for me to minister healing. John didn't receive his physical healing at that time, but the emotional healing to his heart was immense. I pray that God would allow you to tap into the depths of his love as you minister, and that he would break your heart for the people that stand before you in sickness and pain.

OBEDIENCE TO GOD

Bible historians estimate that upwards of three million Israelites left Egypt in the mass exodus led by Moses. After many years of slavery, the Jews suddenly left Egypt. It had been a miraculous few weeks for God's favourite people group leading up to this move.

> The Israelites did just what the Lord commanded Moses and Aaron. At midnight the Lord struck down all the firstborn in Egypt, from the firstborn of Pharaoh, who sat on the throne, to the firstborn of the prisoner, who was in the dungeon, and the firstborn of all the livestock as well. Pharaoh and all his officials and all the Egyptians got up during the night, and there was loud wailing in Egypt, for there was not a house without someone dead. EXODUS 12:28-30

Let's review what happened. Moses returned from exile and announced to Pharaoh that he was going to lead the Israelites out of Egypt and into the promised land. This was obviously met with resistance from the Egyptians, who were using the Jews as slaves. The Jewish slaves were not too happy either when their oppressors increased the workload in response to Moses' demands. God brought a series of plagues upon the Egyptians. Each plague got successively worse, to the point that the oldest son in each Egyptian home died, including Pharaoh's son. Moses was quickly called in to meet with Pharaoh, who gave permission for all the Jews to leave immediately. They literally had just hours to go, and go they did.

As they left, they plundered the nation. They went from house to house and were given the treasures of Egypt. The Egyptians paid the Jews to leave in order to avoid further heartache. As the Israelites left, the Bible says that they walked out of Egypt without faltering (Psalm 105:37).

On the surface this may not mean much, but let me take you back to the condition the slaves would have been in. Out of the three million slaves, most of them would have been malnourished. Many of them would have had diseases. Many of them would have had bruises, lacerations, and other wounds from the beatings they had received from the slave handlers.

The largest recorded healing meeting in the Bible is when these three million people were all instantly healed enough to be able to walk out of Egypt healthy after years of slavery!

How were these folks healed? Through obedience.

They obeyed the instructions God gave them regarding Passover. The people had a choice to do exactly what Moses told them God required, or to take a chance that God really wasn't too concerned about their obedience. Pharaoh and the Egyptians heard the options. The Jewish slaves heard the options. I don't know exactly at what moment the Israelites were healed. It may have been when they put the blood on their doorposts. It may have happened during the Passover meal. It may have happened as they packed their bags and began to leave Egypt.

My personal opinion is that they were healed as they prophetically took the symbols of the Passover. These symbols, as we now know, also prophetically portray Jesus, who became our deliverer and healer. This was to be the very first Passover meal; God gave very clear directives for slaughtering the lamb (what kind of lamb it was to be, how to cook it, where to put its blood). It was almost as if God was giving directions just for the sake of testing their hearts. Would they be obedient? Obedience to God gives life. When God gives directives they are usually for our own benefit, and there are usually consequences to ignoring them.

Let me take you down one other road. The thoughts and impressions that come to us via dreams, journaling, daydreams, etc., may be just the way that God brings healing to us if we obey them. Remember the lady who was healed touching the garment of Jesus (Matthew 9:19-21)? It was a thought that came to her: *If I could just touch his robe.* What if she had not obeyed the Lord and had stayed home that day? Would she have been healed?

Remember the four friends who brought a paralyzed man to Jesus? One of them, perhaps all of them, had a thought: *if we can get him to Jesus, he can be healed.* But, as with almost all revelations from God, there was an obstacle. They couldn't get in the home because of the crowd around the door. One of them had another thought: *let's put him down through the roof!* Their friend got his healing because they listened to their God-thoughts and obeyed them.

Obedience to the written Word of God (*logos* in Greek) and to the revelatory word (*rhema* in Greek) brings healing. In our English translations it is impossible for us to know which of these two root words is used, because both are written as *word*. The good news is that both bring life.

When we receive a word, there is the possibility of a miracle. However God speaks, whether through a revelation or through reading the Bible, there is life in his words. Our part is to obey.

The obedience is where our healing takes place. Jesus knew this and reminded his disciples often that he always did what his Father asked him to (John 5:30). Jesus obeyed the Father.

"I DON'T LIKE"

I often speak at family camps in the United Kingdom. One of them was for the Elim Pentecostal churches in the Liverpool area of England. At the end of my talk, a number of people hung around to have me pray for specific issues. The last lady in line told me about a constant pain in her foot. She couldn't put any pressure on her legs without feeling intense pain on the bottom of her feet. I was feeling good; each person I had ministered to so far had been healed.

My confidence was up and I think the people in line were also feeling it, as they saw one after another walking away healed. But when I placed my hands on her feet, nothing happened. No problem, I tried prayer number two. Prayer one focuses on the anointing for healing. Prayer two focuses on demonic influences. After a couple minutes of nothing I got frustrated and asked the Lord what the blockage was that was keeping this woman from her healing. I heard a short sentence: *I don't like.* I asked her to finish my sentence. I said, "I don't like..."

She immediately said, "Myself."

Bingo. I went on to talk to her about the areas in her life where she was cursing herself. She actually used the word *pressure* when describing how she saw herself. The Lord reminded me that this was also the word she used to talk about the pain in her foot. She was hating herself and putting pressure on herself for some of the circumstances in her life. She was cursing herself and it was showing up in her feet. All the pain in her feet disappeared as she forgave herself.

I have had this happen time and time again. I get a simple thought from God and go with it. As I obey a small thought, it becomes the breakthrough for the person I am ministering to. I had the choice of ignoring the *I don't like* thought, or recognizing that God was speaking to me. As I obeyed his word, this lady had her breakthrough.

When you have opportunity to minister healing, be very careful to listen to the revelatory words that come to you. You will find that there is life in obeying them. While you are listening or ministering, you may feel God leading you to say or ask something specific. He may have you do something. Follow those leadings. When we obey, healing is possible!

In Exodus 15:26 God tells the Israelites:

> *If you listen carefully to the Lord your God and do what is right in his eyes, if you pay attention to his commands and keep all his decrees, I will not bring on you any of the diseases I brought on the Egyptians, for I am the Lord, who heals you.*

This passage happens after the Passover and the exodus from Egypt. With the escape fresh in their minds, and the sounds of agony from the screams and wails of the Egyptians as they woke up to find their first-born children dead, Moses passes on another life lesson to us. It is a very simple one: live according to God's truth and you won't get sick in the first place. If we listen and do what God says, he keeps us from disease. The implication is obvious. God says that he brought diseases on the Egyptians for not listening and obeying.

Healing comes from God. His design is clearly linked to listening and doing. When we don't listen to him, we are actually choosing to move out from under his protection into a place where Satan dominates. Because Pharaoh and the Egyptians were stubborn and did the opposite of what they heard through Moses, all sorts of sickness came to them—even death. When God lifts his hand of protection, Satan quickly moves in to fill the gap. Satan brings pain, disease, and death (John 10:10).

The point that Moses is making, on behalf of God, is that they need to listen carefully to voice of the Lord do what is right in his eyes. Notice again that the passage begins with the conditional word *if*. Listening can keep us from getting sick in the first place. God clearly states, *"I am the Lord, who heals you."* God is the giver of life and when we are connected to him, we receive his life-giving and healing grace. Moses was making a strong point at the crucial time when the Israelites were getting ready to re-establish themselves as a nation after about 430 years in captivity. All of the sickness that they had experienced as they lived in Egypt, all of the sickness that came to the Egyptians during the plagues, all of this would not have happened, if the Israelites had listened to God and done what he said.

I've already stated that healing is easily accessible for all because of what Jesus endured in the beating and the cross. Healing is part of the kingdom, the very nature of God. He is a healing God and shows it throughout the Scriptures, both Old and New Testaments. For those of us who minister healing, I'd like to remind you that while healing is a free gift, it is not cheap. Healing cost God; Jesus was the price. As for us, God requires obedience. He intends for us to remain healthy. Good health is simply linked with listening and doing.

TESTIMONIES IN NIGERIA

Several years ago I had the opportunity to travel to Lagos, Nigeria, to witness the ministry of a certain pastor first-hand. One of the things that stood out in my mind was how strongly he linked obedience with healing, and perhaps more specifically, the lack of obedience with disease. Many of the people who had visible plagues on their bodies were asked to give testimony before they received prayer. We watched a video of one man in the meeting that documented his healing from what they called "body poison." He had this terrible, life-threatening plague on his genitals. When he was asked how this came about, he confessed to being a fornicator and adulterer.

The pastor made a point of warning his congregation that this is the kind of thing that happens when we sin. After the man was ministered to and pronounced healed, he was strongly encouraged to "go and sin no more" (John 5:14 and 8:11). This seemed to be the motto of the church. After each person was ministered to, they were admonished to sin no more. The link between the various diseases and what they had done was clear. Many of the connections were drastic. Sin sexually, and your sexual parts will be plagued. Ouch!

God requires that we listen and do what he says. Healing stays if we don't sin. We stay in health by living according to God's truth. Where does healing power come from? It comes from the very nature of God. His design is that we never get into situations where we bring health problems upon ourselves. Is there disease in heaven? No. Why not? Because we will always listen and do what God wants when we get there.

HEALTH COMES BY STAYING CLOSE TO GOD

Was there sickness in the Garden of Eden? Yes and no. There was no sickness until Adam and Eve chose not to listen to God. They actively decided to disobey him. Because they sinned and then tried to hide from God, their punishment was expulsion from the garden. The garden was a place of God's presence. It was heaven on earth. When they sinned, they took themselves out of God's presence and into the contamination of a world where sin abounds.

Part of our role is to lead people into places of God's presence—where they will have sickness again. I think that the passage from Exodus implies that we can stay healthy all the time; however, this means staying close to the Father and living like Jesus did. There is no record in Scriptures of Jesus being sick. It is absent. We know that he was tired, he was hungry, he was grieved, etc., but he was never sick. Why? Because he always listened to his Father and obeyed God.

This book isn't about nutrition. But I want to say that eating healthy and staying active is very important. Let me also share a couple very interesting verses from Paul. He said to Timothy, "Stop drinking only water, and use a little wine because of your stomach and your frequent illnesses" (1 Timothy 5:23). He was clearly giving some direction on nutritional issues. "For physical training is of some value, but godliness has value for all things, holding promise for both the present life and the life to come" (1 Timothy 4:8). More important than nutrition is valuing godliness. It helps right now and factors into eternity.

There are many negatives penalties that come to our physical bodies when we disobey the teaching of the Scriptures. A great resource for me is a book entitled, A More Excellent Way, by Henry Wright. Wright is famous for quoting the 1 Timothy 4:8 passage and saying, "eating broccoli and running five miles a day isn't going to help you get well if bitterness if killing you."

Pastor Wright seeks to link diseases with potential spiritual laws that we have broken. He uses passages from the scriptures, medical studies, and discernment to come to his conclusions. Let me give you an example: I have battled cholesterol for several years. I have a physical problem that my cardiologist (a former member of our church) has diagnosed. My arteries are thin. That means that any plaque that is building up, will cause heart problems for me quicker than if I had normal veins.

Wright has another idea. When I looked up cholesterol for the first time I was very upset. I took what he wrote personally. I was angry that Wright would even think of saying such a thing about me. What he said was that the probable, note *probable*, cause for cholesterol was self-hatred. Not possible. I'm very comfortable being in my skin. I don't dislike myself. Then I heard God speaking to me: *Would you like my opinion?* Uh-oh. I said yes. He said, *While you love yourself now, what did you think about yourself when you were thirteen? You still haven't repented of that!* He was right. I hated myself back then. I instantly remembered cursing God out loud for being taller than most other kids, for having pimples, and for having thick lenses for my poor eyesight. I quickly repented of my behaviour.

I then looked up high blood pressure. Wright says that this usually is a penalty for worrying. Jesus says not to worry, but I do. I repented of that as well and asked the Lord to help me give him my problems.

I was in to see my family doctor shortly after reading Wright's book and doing the prayer ministry. She took my blood pressure, as she always does. Guess what she said to me? My blood pressure was much lower. She recommended I cut back to half of the medicine that I taking to correct the

SOURCES OF HEALING POWER

problem. She also suggested a four-month vegetarian diet. I followed her advice and a few months later I got a good news and bad news report. The good news was that my blood pressure and cholesterol was better than the last time. The bad news: she wanted me to keep being a vegetarian!

THE NAME OF JESUS

There is power in the name of Jesus. More specifically, there is healing power that comes from the wonderful name of Jesus. Embodied in his name is anointing for healing. Even Peter's critics recognized it. They asked Peter in Acts 4:7–10:

"By what power or what name did you do this?"

Then Peter, filled with the Holy Spirit, said to them: "Rulers and elders of the people! If we are being called to account today for an act of kindness shown to a man who was lame and are being asked how he was healed, then know this, you and all the people of Israel: It is by the name of Jesus Christ of Nazareth, whom you crucified but whom God raised from the dead, that this man stands before you healed.

I love this passage. These verses from Acts are ones that I teach from often because they summarize a very important truth. The background is seen in Acts 3 where Peter and John have raised a crippled man, who had been that way for 40 years. This is their first recorded miracle in their own anointing. (They had healed the sick in Matthew 10 under a borrowed anointing, when Jesus had sent them out to heal the sick.) As a consequence of healing the crippled man, Peter gets to preach to thousands of people in the temple courts, and a couple thousand get saved.

However, this doesn't go down well with the Jewish leaders, and Peter and John are subsequently arrested. They spend the night in jail and the next morning they have their court appearance. The last thing that the Sanhedrin wanted to hear was that the healing was related to Jesus. These were the same men who, months earlier, had demanded that Jesus be crucified.

They had dealt with the "Jesus" problem, but now there were two more problems, who were doing the same things as Jesus had done. The Sanhedrin was seeking to rid the city from what they saw as a heresy: the teaching that Jesus was the Christ, the Messiah. Roman soldiers had already been paid bribe money to shut up and deny the resurrection. They were not about to let some Galilean fishermen further damage their stronghold on the people. The leaders needed to make a strong statement against Peter and John, or they were in trouble. What they wanted to hear from Peter and John was that they had healed this man through magic, Buddha, Mohammed, or any name but that of Jesus.

As they asked how the disciples healed, the leaders prepared themselves for the worst. Peter, speaking under the anointing of the Holy Spirit, was to the point. This miracle was performed because of the name of Jesus. Names carry power; wonderful for us, but not so wonderful for the Jewish leaders. The Sanhedrin also knew this, which is why they specifically said, *"By what power or what name did you do this?"*

Remember what Peter and John spoke over the lame man? They said they didn't have money to give but, *"in the name of Jesus Christ of Nazareth, get up and walk"* (Acts 3:6). Not bad for their first try at healing. Where did the healing anointing come from? The anointing came by invoking the name of Jesus. The name of Jesus is very special. There are many names that Jesus had and each is significant. But let's focus on the two most common.

Jesus is the name given to him by his parents Mary and Joseph. It means saviour. When the angel came and announced to Mary that she would give birth, the angel specifically said to name him Jesus because he would save his people (Matthew 1:21). The word *save* is *sozo* in the Greek language. *Sozo* is used in the account of Jesus, not just to refer to salvation, but also to refer to his healing and deliverance ministry. It is an all-encompassing word that means heal, save, do well, and deliver. When we use his name, we invoke all those qualities.

The second name is the word *Christ*. Christ means Anointed One, and was also translated as Messiah. The Messiah, the Anointed One, comes to bring hope, freedom, deliverance, healing, and life. One of the most profound days in the life of Jesus' followers was when they realized that Jesus actually was the Messiah. As such, he was anointed in everything he did. His name meant that he could do no wrong.

Now imagine what happened when Peter used both names as he spoke to the crippled man, *"in the name of Jesus Christ"* (Acts 3:6). The power that was unleashed by saying these names together was synergized. Inherent in the name Jesus Christ is healing power. Peter and John were very happy to tell the Sanhedrin that this was how the man now stood before them fully healed. The Jewish leaders were helpless; they had met an unstoppable force. As Gamaliel explained in Acts 5:39, as a leadership group they were fighting against God.

MAYBE DEAD?

I love to travel to Africa. It is one of my favourite destinations for a multitude of reasons. Not only did I grow up in Malawi, but there is just something about the colour of the ground, the smells of the plants, the warmth of the wind, that speaks to me.

On our last trip to Mozambique, Sandra and I had a small team with us, including Ragnhild, who is a nurse from Germany, and Sarah, who is a financial advisor and a member of Catch The Fire Toronto. For most, the highlight of their time in serving with Iris Ministries in Pemba, Mozambique, is a trip to the bush. Let me explain what it means to be in the bush. The word *bush* in Africa means remote. An area where there is no electricity, no toilets, and often no visible water sources. In Mozambique, it means that many of the people living in these areas are isolated. They have never been to a city. They haven't seen a movie, talked on a cell phone, or seen a person who doesn't have black skin. They often have never heard of the name of Jesus.

What happens on most outings is a team from Iris arrives and sets up a generator in a very public area within a village. As the others on the team arrive, they quickly set up tents where they will be sleeping overnight. Once the darkness sets in, the *Jesus* movie is played in the local language. For most, this is their first time seeing a movie. The people from the village all come and sit in the dust or stand behind the children. Over the three-hour movie, people continue to arrive from the bush. After the movie, the crowd are introduced to Jesus through a short sermon. The people are told that the same Jesus is able to heal their diseases. A ministry time begins and most teams get to see someone healed of blindness or deafness. It happens every week. Many of the people give their lives to Jesus after the talk. The movie makes sense to them and causes them to turn from their tribal religion. They have great smiles on their faces as they embrace new truth.

So the last time in Mozambique, Sandra and I didn't go into the bush. Our team went without us, including Sarah and Ragnhild. After a night sleeping in a tent, the team was up very early. They had a quick breakfast and then began to go from hut to hut to talk to the people and minister to them. Sarah and Ragnhild were teamed together. They noticed a body wrapped in blankets off the edge of the village. They were told that it was a lady who was either dead or about to die. I think the uncertainty as to whether the lady was dead provoked them. They went to investigate.

They started by talking to the wrapped body. No response. They were told she was deaf. If she was alive, she wouldn't hear them. That meant they needed to unwrap her. Sure enough the lady was still alive but very dehydrated. Sarah and Ragnhild prayed for her health, her hearing, and for her recovery. As they brought Heidi Baker towards the lady, they saw her reach for a water container they had left with her. That meant she was now able to see! Heidi joined them in ministering to the African woman. Within minutes she was hearing! They trimmed her nails, combed her hair, and presented her back to the village in much better health. How did this dying lady receive her healing? The name of Jesus.

Friends, when we minister on behalf of God we are allowed and welcomed to invoke the wonderful name of Jesus Christ. Anointed Saviour is another way to say his name. There is healing power that is released as we honour this name that is full of life. Please be sure to use the name of Jesus Christ when you minister. His name carries an anointed punch and brings healing to all. He is the master representative of God, and being in very nature God, his name brings healing.

Let me bless you as you use his name in ministry:

Father, the most wonderful name in history is that of your Son, Jesus Christ. Thank you that you are not only willing for us to share in your ministry, but you also allow us to use the name of Jesus. Father thank you that the name of Jesus carries authority and power. Thank you that at the name of Jesus, we are able to heal the sick, command pain to leave someone's body, and restore health to your people. Father, I bless my friend to be a wonderful carrier of the name of Jesus Christ. In his name I pray, amen.

CHAPTER 3

The Healing Power of Faith

Just then a woman who had been subject to bleeding for twelve years came up behind him and touched the edge of his cloak. She said to herself, "If I only touch his cloak, I will be healed." Jesus turned and saw her. "Take heart, daughter," he said, "your faith has healed you." And the woman was healed at that moment.

MATTHEW 9:20-22

I love this passage! There are so many principles of healing in this story that you could spend all day here. With that said, the key message in this story is that faith allows us to be healed.

Here was a lady who had been bleeding for twelve years. The other accounts of this story, in Mark and Luke, add that she had spent all of her money on doctors and continued to get worse. Men, we can't imagine what she went through, but to state the bare truth, she was having an unending monthly period. She was in pain, suffering, bleeding, and couldn't find anyone to help her. Then she heard that Jesus was in town. A thought crossed her mind: *What if I could just touch his clothes?*

Friends, these kinds of thoughts are filled with the possibility of faith. Why? Because they are inspired by the Holy Spirit. God has just whispered something and we've caught it. Let me give you my simplified take on how faith works. Hope and faith are strongly related. Hope is wonderful, but faith is better!

In this narrative, hope comes via a thought or revelation. Hope may have given her some emotional strength, but she still wasn't healed. Faith is the step after hope. Faith is acting on our hope. For this lady, faith was doing what she heard from God—actually going to Jesus and touching his clothes. It was the touch that healed her. Her hope became faith, and her faith caused her to be healed!

Let me ask you a simple question. Did Jesus heal her, or did her faith in touching the hem of his garment heal her? Jesus was actually oblivious to what was going on. In essence, she healed herself. Yes, Jesus was the object of her faith, and yes, she tapped into the anointing on his life. Can I suggest that if the lady had been told by God to touch a leper and she did, she would be healed. It was her acting in faith that brought the miracle.

In the companion passages of Mark and Luke, we read that Jesus felt something supernatural happen to him when she touched him. He felt power leaving his body. Being in a large crowd, he turned to find out who had just tapped into God's anointing for healing. His disciples thought him a bit crazy for asking the question and pointed out that everyone was touching him. But Jesus knew that one touch was different than the grabs and pats on his back from the rest of the crowd. One touch was a healing touch, the other were touches from people who treated him as a celebrity. They would go home to brag to their friends about how they had both seen and touched Jesus.

MIRACLES IN THE DESERT

One of the most amazing miracles I have witnessed came about because of a thought. I was in a refugee camp outside of Khartoum, Sudan, with one of our connect leaders, Brian Girdwood, visiting an Iris orphanage that one of the women from our church in Toronto was leading.

As part of our week there, we had four open-air crusades in the middle of the refugee camp. Each day we had said that on the fourth day we would be feeding everyone a burger and a soda. On day four the crowds were double the size. The meeting took place under the sun in more than forty-degree Celsius heat. Each meeting consisted of a simple sermon on God's ability to heal followed by a two- to three-hour ministry time. There were about four of us praying: Brian, our host Maria, a pastor from South Sudan, and myself.

We tried to get people into lines for prayer but that plan quickly went out the window. We found ourselves in the crowd with people all around. People were either being healed or simply leaving after we ministered. It was really hard to know, as we didn't have translators; they were off ministering and doing better than us! From time to time we saw a smile and through gestures found out a person was healed. Everyone who had a major healing was taken to the microphone by Maria and was given the opportunity to tell their story.

Most the people in this refugee camp were Muslims who were on the run from Darfur. A few were from the conflict in what was then the south of Sudan. My recollection is that the crowd was mostly women, children, and seniors. The men were either fighting or dead. Each person gave credit to Jesus as the source of their healing.

After about four hours of preaching, ministry, altar calls, and more ministry, it was time to serve the food. We had people gather around a small tent we'd set up. It was there to provide shade for some of the senior women, and to be a focal point for our crusade. Just as I was about to give thanks to Jesus for the food, I had a thought enter my mind to tell everyone the story of the ten lepers who were healed on their way to Jerusalem after a meeting Jesus (Luke 17).

Despite that fact that we had stopped ministering, that the food was ready, that people were once again relatively orderly, and that we were tired and hot, I decided to act on the thought. I stopped giving instructions about the food and told the story of how the lepers were healed on their way home. I asked each person who hadn't yet been healed to put their hands on the part of the their body that needed a touch from God.

I began to pray and was immediately interrupted by a scream from the widow's tent behind me. The other women brought a lady towards us. She was in her seventies. She was given the microphone and told the people that when she was a small child she was playing in water and woke up blind in both eyes the next day. She said that water spirits caused her blindness. (Water spirits are very real and cause great physical problems. They are mentioned in the Bible with names such as Leviathan.)

She told the crowd that when she put her hands on her eyes, both of her eyes were instantly healed and now she could see perfectly. Wow! We delayed the food for another half hour as we prayed for more people to be healed and gave people another chance to invite Jesus into their lives. The point of the story is that healing came as the result of a spontaneous thought that interrupted me. I was talking about food when a Bible story came to my mind, and I acted on it.

GOD-THOUGHTS ARE OPPORTUNITIES FOR BREAKTHROUGH

Can I encourage you that this is how God often communicates. Random thoughts are often God-thoughts that have the potential to bring healing, financial, and relationship breakthroughs. Friend, you can literally heal yourself if you will act in faith on the things that God has spoken into your life. If you haven't felt that God has said anything specific to you, then you can take what he has spoken to you through the Bible. Begin to act on the thoughts that come to you when you read this book. Don't give in to doubt and question random thoughts. Don't dismiss them. Complacency is one of the curses over many of our lives. We simply have to get up and go do what God knows is possible.

The woman who had a bleeding condition for twelve years was healed because she acted on a daring thought. She did not care that others were around. She didn't care that the customs of her culture dictated that she was unclean and was supposed to stay away from crowds. All that mattered was that after twelve years of suffering and having spent all her money, she could be healed. She was also desperate enough to take a chance that her thought was actually a God-thought. Why was she healed? Because her thought was rooted in God. He wanted her healed.

One of Satan's primary strategies is to steal faith from God's people. He does this by challenging God-thoughts. As soon as we get an idea, we get second thoughts. Satan partners with our unsanctified mind to convince us that the idea doesn't make sense. This is why it is so important to be renewing our mind (Romans 12:1–2).

Our personal history also works against us. Most of us, probably all of us, have had disappointments. We've been to healing meetings. We've said the prayers. We've sent an offering to the televangelist. We've acted when we thought it was God. We've seen friends suffer from sickness. We've seen loved ones die from a disease way before it was their time. We remind ourselves that we've been down this road before and it didn't work. Combined with a lack of faith and negative history, we hear from others who have also not been healed. Why should we believe?

Perhaps our biggest challenge is that our spirit has usually been crushed or wounded (Psalm 34:18, Proverbs 17:22, 18:14). Our culture is so focused on rationalism that we've had our spirit turned to the *off* position. We've done this to ourselves by believing lies and by doubting. Others have also influenced us. Their lack of faith greatly hinders our spirit. People have made fun of us when we have had a thought that differs from the norm. Parents have told us that our dreams don't pay the bills. We've allowed our spirit, the very part of us that God primarily connects with, to be told to shut up. We've shut ourselves off when something hasn't "made sense." Revelation isn't supposed to make sense. Our mind is going to be in conflict with God's thoughts! Once we understand this battle, we can start to win.

Here is a quick advertisement for another ministry. Arthur Burk is way ahead of anyone else I know on the topic of developing and nurturing your spirit. He has great resources available on his website (theslg.com) that will help get your spirit back to its rightful place as leader over your mind and your soul.

Will you begin to live by faith? Begin to act on everything that God says to you regarding your healing. Your faith can make you well.

THE FAITH OF OTHERS CAN HEAL ME

Not only does your faith move mountains of sickness and pain, but the faith of those around you does too. Consider Matthew 9:2–8:

> Some men brought to him a paralyzed man, lying on a mat. When Jesus saw
> their faith, he said to the man, "Take heart, son; your sins are forgiven." At this,
> some of the teachers of the law said to themselves, "This fellow is blasphem-
> ing!" Knowing their thoughts, Jesus said, "Why do you entertain evil thoughts
> in your hearts? Which is easier: to say, 'Your sins are forgiven,' or to say, 'Get

up and walk'? But I want you to know that the Son of Man has authority on earth to forgive sins." So he said to the paralyzed man, "Get up, take your mat and go home." Then the man got up and went home. When the crowd saw this, they were filled with awe; and they praised God, who had given such authority to man.

The principle I'd like to focus on is that the faith of others inspired Jesus to action. When Jesus saw the faith of the four friends, he began to minister and pronounced both forgiveness and healing. A great healing happened largely because of the faith of friends. In Matthew's account, Jesus was the agent for the healing, but it was the faith of the friends that activated the process. The meeting doesn't appear to have been a healing meeting, but a scheduled discussion with Jewish leaders. When Jesus saw the four men lowering this man into the crowded room, he jumped into action.

These guys on the roof have great confidence that God wants this man healed. I'll partner with them to see it happen. I think this is the kind of thought that came to Jesus. What was it that these four men had faith in? Can I suggest that one of them, perhaps all of them, were acting on a God-thought. It probably went like this: the four of them were having coffee when one guy said, "I had a dream last night that Johnny was walking. I took him to see Jesus and he was instantly healed." My guess is when one of them shared his idea, the others chimed in with their ideas.

"Hey, I had a dream like that for Johnny a couple weeks ago!"

Coffee was now the last thing on their minds, as they quickly realized that they all believed that God wanted their friend healed. The fact that Jesus was in town only added to their enthusiasm. The only problem, Jesus was in a private meeting with all the big shots from their region. Not to be disheartened, one of them suggests that they do something stupid.

"Let's tear open the roof!" They look at each other and briefly think about the consequences.

"Why not, what's the worst that can happen?" Off they go to get Johnny into the room.

As a group, they acted on someone's hope. At least one of them believed that a miracle could happen if they did something. I've found that often my faith is stronger for someone else than it is for myself. It is easier to believe for others than it is to believe that a miracle can happen to me. You've probably noticed the same. God really doesn't seem to care where the faith originates, as long as someone has faith. God wants to partner with somebody, anybody! This is how many healing miracles take place.

FAITH ADDED TO FAITH

You may remember hearing about the story of a Nigerian pastor who died in a car accident. His body was taken to the hospital where his family doctor pronounced him dead. He was embalmed with formaldehyde in preparation for the funeral, which was to take place in a couple days. Three different doctors verified his death. His wife had a thought. What if she took him to a church meeting where Reinhard Bonnke was scheduled to preach? Reinhard would raise her husband from the dead! (For those of you who don't know about Reinhard, he has led more people to Jesus than anyone in history.)

When she got to the church they would not allow her to take his body into the main meeting. She insisted, but no one would let her do what she wanted to do. The body was taken instead to a basement room and placed on a table. One of the assistant pastors somehow heard about the lady and her story. He joined his faith with hers and he began to minister to the dead pastor.

The prayer ministry was caught on videotape. It shows how his body began to breath again, even though he was still dead. The pastor and wife began to massage his neck and his head began to move. Then all of a sudden, he jumped up—alive! His resurrection is on YouTube. I was with Reinhard recently and asked him about the pastor. He verified that he was still alive and made two interesting points. First, the resurrected man's body smelled of formaldehyde for months. Second, despite the fact that there was no blood in the body when he was raised from the dead, he is perfectly healthy and has fathered two more children.

Whose faith brought this man back to life? It was his wife's! The assistant pastor also believed it was possible and added his faith to the mix. The dead man obviously wasn't a part of the process, as dead people don't have any faith.

The Bible says, *"if two of you on earth agree about anything they ask for, it will be done for them by my Father in heaven"* (Matthew 18:19). We can touch God and activate miracles for others and ourselves simply by agreeing in faith. Can I encourage you to ask God to bring people into your life who will have faith for your healing? If you don't think you have enough faith, get friends who do. Remember, God doesn't seem to care who has the faith as long as someone does!

MIRACULOUS FAITH

Healings are amazing, but miracles are much better. My understanding of a divine healing is when God steps in and speeds up the timeline for a person's recovery. Medicine and surgery may be able to help, but God does it faster, often instantly. A miracle is when God steps in and does something that simply can't be done. Medicine is not going to bring a person back from the dead. God wants us to have faith for both healing and miracles.

While he [Jesus] was saying this, a synagogue leader came and knelt before him and said, "My daughter has just died. But come and put your hand on her, and she will live." Jesus got up and went with him, and so did his disciples ... When Jesus entered the synagogue leader's house and saw the noisy crowd and people playing pipes, he said, "Go away. The girl is not dead but asleep." But they laughed at him. After the crowd had been put outside, he went in and took the girl by the hand, and she got up. News of this spread through all that region. MATTHEW 9:18-19, 23-26

Wow, this story encourages us to believe in the impossible. Here we have the first of three stories where Jesus raises someone from the dead. Being that this is the first story of a resurrection, there are lots of interesting points to be made, most of them relating to faith. Let's first look at who this father is. In this account he is introduced as a ruler, but when you look at the expanded versions in Mark and Luke, we find out that his name is Jairus and that he is the ruler of a synagogue.

The ruler of the synagogue was not a rabbi, priest, or teacher, but rather the president of the meeting place. He would be the like chairman of a board of directors or the president of an organization. My speculation is that with this role, he would probably not have been an active follower of Jesus; in fact, he may have been a detractor, as many of the leading Jews were. He probably was wealthy. Usually wealthy people get the honour and prestige of being the synagogue ruler, even today.

Here is what I love about this story: even though he probably was not a follower of Jesus, when push came to shove and his twelve-year-old daughter died, Jairus knew to turn to him. He found Jesus, and in an act of humility he bowed and asked Jesus for the impossible. Jairus was asking for a miracle the likes of which the nation of Israel had not seen in centuries. The last recorded person to be raised from the dead in the Scriptures was a man who was accidentally buried on the bones of Elisha (2 Kings 13:21). In almost a millennium no one had been resurrected from the dead. But that is just what Jairus wants and believes for.

Why does he come to Jesus for such a miracle? Jairus had not only heard the stories of what Jesus had done, but he had probably witnessed some of them as well. Being from Capernaum, he was probably a friend of the royal official (mayor) whose son was healed by Jesus via long distance (John 4:46). Jairus would also have known the centurion we see in Luke 7 and Matthew 8, who was the chief of police in Capernaum. Jairus may not have liked him, being a Roman and all, but he would have heard how the centurion's servant who was paralyzed and in great pain had been healed without a visit to the home. Jairus knew that if his daughter was to live again, the only hope was an encounter with Jesus. While the story doesn't say where his faith came from, my guess is that either he or his wife had a God-thought that their little girl could live again. So off to Jesus he went. Remember, faith is taking a hope and putting it into action.

I love how Jesus responded. It is the same response that Jesus had to every single person who came to him. He immediately said yes to the request. Jesus saw a man with faith for a miracle. Jesus was always motivated by the faith of others. He never stopped to pray and ask his Father if this was a good idea. Despite that Jesus had not yet raised someone from the dead, he headed to Jairus' home. It doesn't seem to bother him in the least that a dead girl is slightly harder to heal than a headache! He instinctively knew that God was miraculous God and that in front of him was a man with corresponding faith.

DOUBT IS THE ENEMY OF OUR MIRACLES

Those of you who know this story well will know that Matthew doesn't tell us the full story. Luke tells us that there was two parts to this story.

The first part, that Matthew misses, is that Jairus comes to Jesus while his daughter is still alive. Jesus agrees to go and touch her, but the crowds come and slow him down. Not only that, but Jesus stops walking after he senses someone has been healed. It turns out that it is a woman who was bleeding for twelve years. A great miracle, but not great timing for Jairus, who needs to get Jesus to his home while his daughter is still alive. Luke tells us that while Jairus waits for Jesus to finish with this lady, a couple of his friends come and give the worst news possible: *"your daughter is dead"* (Mark 5:35).

Imagine the wave of doubt that Jairus must have faced. Most of us would give up at this point. Luke tells us that in the face of overwhelming circumstances (a dead daughter, no resurrections in over 1000 years), Jesus tells Jairus to *"just believe"* (Mark 5:36).

When Jesus got to the house he was met with a second wave of doubt. Jesus, knowing that doubt is the enemy of faith, got rid of every doubting person as quick as he could. The mourners who had already gathered were pushed aside. It would appear that even some of his disciples were doubting and excluded from the bedroom. (It may also be that there simply wasn't room for all twelve to be in the house. I've been to Capernaum and the ruins of the ancient houses suggest that most homes were the size of our kitchens!) Jesus, Peter, John, and James, along with Jairus and his wife, were the only ones in the room with the dead girl.

Jesus spoke a word of faith over her in Mark 5:41. *"Talitha koum!"* which means, "Little girl, I say to you, get up!" The Bible says that immediately she got up and walked. Not bad for his first resurrection!

MIRACLE IN AMSTERDAM

Let me tell you a story that I don't often share. In 1999, I led the first team from our church to Mozambique to visit Rolland and Heidi Baker. They were not famous then; they were simply looking after one orphanage and doing church at a garbage dump. On the way there we had a stopover in Amsterdam, where I had the opportunity to preach at a Pentecostal church on the Sunday. At the very end of my sermon and just as I was about to give an altar call for people to connect with Jesus, something happened at the back of the church.

I noticed people standing and looking down. I ask the pastor to check to see what had happened because I could see trauma on the faces of several people. He went to the back and came to the front of the church crying. He said that a lady had just died. Others in the congregation who knew the lady also began to weep. Sorrow and defeat entered the atmosphere of this church gathering in an instant. It was sad how quickly all hope was drained from the believers who had gathered there to worship God and grow in their Christian faith.

I still had my lapel microphone on and I began to do what I felt God asking me to do. I prayed for a resurrection. I prayed out loud while the pastor sat in the front row crying, along with the congregation. I challenged the people to begin to pray, to speak in Dutch, in English, and in tongues if they knew how. Slowly they did. At the same time, three nurses who were a part of the meeting began to give the dead woman mouth-to-mouth resuscitation.

Later, I heard that two of the nurses, who were sitting behind the woman, said they heard her last breath leave her body. They recognized this sound and used their skills to try to restore her life. They said she had no pulse, no heartbeat, and was not breathing. They pounded her chest to reactivate her heart. I kept praying out loud, commanding the spirit of death to leave, speaking life into her body, etc. One of the men on our mission team, Keld

Pederson, grabbed his video camera and began to film. He was told to stop by those around the lady, as they didn't want this to be filmed.

I can't remember how long we prayed, but after about five minutes the lady was resuscitated. I can't say that she was raised from the dead, as there was no official death certificate and no doctors to confirm it. What I do know is that the nurses said that she was dead and came back. Either way, something good happened!

Some of you need a miracle. For some of you, a thought has come into your spirit as you are reading this chapter that says a miracle can happen to you. Continue to believe. Continue to hold to the truth that God has spoken to you. Miracles do happen. God has not changed; he continues to be the very same God he was when Jesus was walking on earth!

THE PRAYER OF FAITH

The prayer of faith is a powerful prayer that James, the leader of the first church in Jerusalem, said would make a sick person well. This prayer of faith is a command, not a request.

> Is anyone among you sick? Let them call the elders of the church to pray over them and anoint them with oil in the name of the Lord. And the prayer offered in faith will make the sick person well; the Lord will raise them up. If they have sinned, they will be forgiven. JAMES 5:14-15

The point James is making is that prayers uttered in faith are supposed to work. By implication, prayers that aren't accompanied by faith don't work and don't bring healing. A simple way to know if the prayer is spoken in faith is if the person gets well. The emphasis in this passage is on the person who is ministering, rather than the person who is sick. The only thing that the sick person needs to believe is that spiritual people can help. Remember, faith already knows what God wants and simply agrees with him. It's doing what you know to be true even when you don't see it in front of you.

Do you remember the story where the disciples had enough faith to wake up Jesus? They were in a boat during a storm, fearing for their lives. While they didn't have enough faith to quiet the storm, they did have faith that Jesus could. Jesus called that *"little faith"* (Matthew 8:26). Little faith still gets the storm to stop but it isn't as dramatic and life-changing as being the one doing the miracle. When I don't need Jesus to be around for the miracle to happen, that is called *"great faith"* (Matthew 8:10).

The same principle exists in James. Our part is to have a beginner's level of faith and agree that the elders can help with our healing. The elders' responsibility is to pray with faith. Many of you have heard stories of people who have been told by well-meaning friends or Christian leaders that they lacked the faith necessary to receive their healing. While there may be an element of truth in that, the chances are that the person who ministered may not have had enough faith either.

I'll admit that many times when I am praying for someone, doubt creeps in and I begin to think, *I don't know about this one.* I'm sure you've been in that place too. There are many times when I'm secretly thinking, *God, I need your faithfulness to override me for this person.*

HITTING THE WALL

I remember being asked by John Arnott at our Catch The Fire conference, in 2003, to lead a healing component at one of the evening meetings. During the worship I felt God say to me, *this is a night of miracles.* I had been asking God for a word and clearly felt that he spoke to me. I knew this was going to be good!

When I took to the platform there was expectancy, but not to the level that matched what God wanted to do. I prayed for all the people that stood for healing. We had the folks nearby lay hands on each other. After a few minutes, I asked for testimonies of those who had been healed. We had some good healings but I knew that God had said to go for the miraculous. None of those giving testimony were sharing miracles, just simple healings. I pushed in again. I asked those who were in pain or battling sickness not to give up, as many of them were now seated. We prayed once more and sure enough, better healings began to happen. I invited people to come to the front and share their miracle.

A Japanese pastor brought two people from his group forward. Both were in wheelchairs. Both were able to stand to their feet after the second round of prayer. Finally this was heading in the direction God had spoken to me about; miracles were happening. I was ready to push even further and see dramatic signs and wonders. I was on a roll! I asked the Japanese pastor to have the first man walk a few steps and he did. Everyone clapped. Wonderful! I then asked him to have the next lady stand again and begin to walk. He explained to me that she couldn't walk, to which I said, "That is why I'm asking her to try to walk." He reiterated that she couldn't walk. I began to get frustrated; I felt that if she began to take a few steps her healing would increase. I felt that this pastor, who was also her translator, was in my way.

The pastor then explained to me off microphone why he was saying she couldn't walk. He told me that she only had one leg. The other one had been amputated many years ago and instead of a hard prosthetic she only had Styrofoam under her trousers. She literally had no support to walk with. It would be impossible for her to walk unless God gave her a new leg. All of a sudden, I remembered again what God said to me about this being a night for miracles. God again spoke to me at that instant. He asked me to believe for this lady to have a new leg. This was the miracle he had talked to me about minutes earlier. What would you do?

I panicked.
I gave in to doubt!

"There is no way that this is going to happen!" I said to myself. Instead of believing and praying in faith for a new leg to grow, I chickened out and left her with the pastor. No one else heard the conversation. No one else knew that she only had one leg. All the conference knew was that she had just testified to standing after many years. No one knew what was going on inside me. My faith had hit a wall. My bravado was not faith at all. I was shown for what I was; a doubter!

Neither the crowd of thousands, nor the pastor, nor this Japanese lady had any idea of the battle that raged in me for those few seconds. All of my insecurities and unbelief seemed to jump up and steal my faith. Sadly, I gave in to them. I was the problem, not the lady. She did have faith to try to stand. She did have faith to tell her pastor that something had happened. She did have faith to come to the front of the crowd and share her story.

James says that the prayer of faith will make you well. The good news is that I have grown in authority since I prayed for that lady. I still hit the wall, but not nearly as often. As a result I've seen great miracles through my prayers of faith! If you need healing, your part in the prayer of faith is to simply ask for prayer. Expect that your elders or prayer team will have more faith than I did that night.

GOD HONOURS HUMILITY

When Jairus asked Jesus to come and touch his dying daughter, he had to humble himself. If he didn't acknowledge his need, his daughter would not have had her miracle.

When the royal official tracked down Jesus in the Galilean hills and asked him to come to Capernaum to heal his son, he had to humble himself. If he had not honoured Jesus, his son would have stayed in the terrible pain.

When Naaman, the general, took off his clothes and bathed in full sight of his soldiers, he had to humble himself. If there were no humility on his part, he would not have been healed.

I'm not trying to put your church leaders on a pedestal. I'm saying that we should not make healing ministers like Reinhard Bonnke or Benny Hinn into demigods. God loves humility and honour. When we get low, he gets high. When we acknowledge our needs, he is able to meet them. When we submit to leaders, he uses the gifts he placed in them for our benefit.

BATTLING FAMILIARITY

When we've been on a long journey to healing, we can face the challenge of familiarity. We think, *my pastor has prayed already for me and nothing happened. In fact, he/she has prayed many times and I'm still not better.* We begin to get disillusioned. This is another test of humility. Will we obey scripture passages such as James 5 when we feel that we've already done that and it didn't work?

Familiarity can also be a pitfall for the church leader. Imagine if you are the pastor of a church and at every healing service you lead, the same people show up and leave as they came in. The challenge for those who are sick is to call out for help. The challenge for the leader is to believe that God can use them regardless of what has or has not happened.

We all have a choice when it comes to faith, whether it's ours, or the faith of friends and families for us. We need to choose to respond. When someone speaks to us what he or she believes to be a word of faith, the potential for healing now transfers to us. We need to agree and do what they have said. Our choice to participate is an act of faith. We act, based on their faith. One of the challenges in this process is often the person who has the word is someone we dismiss, overlook, or ignore.

Now a man who was lame from birth was being carried to the temple gate called

Beautiful, where he was put every day to beg from those going into the temple
courts. When he saw Peter and John about to enter, he asked them for money.
Peter looked straight at him, as did John. Then Peter said, "Look at us!" So the
man gave them his attention, expecting to get something from them. Then Peter
said, "Silver or gold I do not have, but what I do have I give you. In the name of
Jesus Christ of Nazareth, walk." Taking him by the right hand, he helped him
up, and instantly the man's feet and ankles became strong. He jumped to his
feet and began to walk. Then he went with them into the temple courts, walking
and jumping, and praising God. ACTS 3:2-8

In this passage, as in other passages, a word is spoken that has healing
power. Peter commanded the forty-year-old man to get up. If he didn't agree
to being pulled to his feet, he would have remained paralyzed. Because
this man acted on the word, his healing came to him in an instant. The
choice was his to make: receive the word into his spirit and act, or doubt
and do nothing. The crazy thing is that most of us have nothing to lose by
responding to someone's word. There was nothing to be gained by this man
thinking, *These guys are crazy!* Yet sadly, many people miss their healing by
not responding.

I remember a particular Sunday night very distinctly. We had invited a
well-known healing minister to our church. There had been several great
healings already that week and the crowds were much larger than usual.
My guess is that we had upwards of three thousand in the building. The
minister spoke with confidence in everything he said. He spoke and acted
as if God wanted people healed. He was moving in great authority and
people were being healed right before our eyes.

At one point the pastor began to move into the aisles. He saw a lady who had crutches. I recognized the lady. She attended another congregation, but had a Christian ministry in our city and was a friend of our ministry. I had very briefly spoken to her at the beginning of the meeting as she hobbled in. She told me of the healings she seen the previous night. She said she was hoping for a miracle for herself. The infirmity she had made walking difficult, hence her need for crutches. The speaker, seeing her need or led by the Holy Spirit (or both), went to her. He spoke to her and asked her to stand.

Now, in the natural she would be able to stand, either by using the support of her crutches or by grabbing hold of the chair in front of her. She stands every day, but always needs the help of her crutches to walk. Her response was awkward. She told the speaker that she couldn't stand. I think he understood what she meant (that without assistance she couldn't walk), and he again asked her to stand. He didn't care how she got up; he just wanted her to stand so that he could minister to her.

Again, she responded, "I can't stand!" In my spirit, and in talking to others around the room afterwards, we all sensed the same thing. This lady, though she said she wanted to be healed, was not willing to partner with his word of faith. Perhaps she was expecting to be healed another way. Whatever her reason, she stayed in her chair, not even trying to get up.

The speaker, who had a strong personality, gave her a public rebuke. He told her that if she had stood, with or without the aid of crutches, she would have been healed right there and then. Ouch!

He went on to teach the crowd about this very topic. He said, "When some-one who is under the anointing of the Holy Spirit speaks faith into your life, you need to respond." He told us that we needed to trust the "man of God," (especially when he is on a roll as this guy was). Sadly, this lady left the building the same way she came in. I know that the grace of God will give her another chance, but my point is that we need to agree with God when he wants to minister to us through another person.

When Jesus told the ten lepers in Luke 17:12–14 to go and show themselves to the priests, the lepers turned and went. The Bible says that on the way they were healed. They were not healed when Jesus spoke the word. It was when they were obedient to what was spoken to them and began to walk away that they were healed. Priests in Jesus' day lived only in Jerusalem. From Galilee, where the lepers were, to Jerusalem was a three-day walk. There was lots of time for them to have second thoughts, to give up, and to talk themselves out of what Jesus had told them to do.

GRANOLA CHRISTIANS: FLAKES, NUTS AND FRUIT

Bill Johnson, leader of Bethel church in Redding, California, gave a great sermon at our church a couple years ago. His premise was that God pur-posely makes it hard for us to receive from other people. He said that God deliberately uses people that we tend to judge, despise, overlook, etc. God loves to humble us. He loves to put us in situations where we have to forgive, where we need to repent for judging, where we should reconcile, etc. God is always about reconciliation. God is always about honour. God is always about using the weak to confound the strong. God loves to use broken pieces to mend others.

I know none of you feel this way, but here goes: I actually feel that I've come a long way. I know I used to be broken. I know that I was immature and naïve. But, I'm not there now. And that is one of my biggest challenges. Yes, I have matured. Yes, I have grown in my understanding of how the gifts and anointing of the spirit work. Yes, God uses me in my preaching and healing ministry. My battle is not insecurity and feelings of rejection. It is the very opposite. I have to learn to humble myself to others who are not like me and yet seem to have the word of the Lord for any given moment.

Bill told some funny stories of hurting, flaky people being the very ones that God uses in his life. All of us are there. All of us either look down on ourselves or we look down on others. Neither is right nor godly. I need to learn that God can and does use people whom I wouldn't expect. It is a part of the Christian experience to live life not knowing who is a miracle worker in the bodysuit of a wounded soul. I love it and am getting better at this part of life.

My desire for you today is that you will always be responsive to words of faith that others speak to you. Be responsive as well to the thoughts that God gives you. Remember faith comes by hearing the word of God (Romans 10:17). As I pointed out in the previous chapter, the root for *word* in this passage is the Greek word *rhema*, which means revelatory word. It is not the word *logos* referring to the written words of God. Faith comes when you and I respond to the thoughts, impressions, and senses that we get. Just getting them doesn't heal. The doing of the word is what activates and carries the anointing. Always be a doer when you receive a word of faith!

GOD'S FAITHFULNESS

I know what some of you may be thinking. *What if I don't have even a little bit of faith? What if none of my friends have faith? What if the person who is praying for me isn't able to pray in faith?*

Here's what Romans 3:3-4 says: "*What if some were unfaithful? Will their unfaithfulness nullify God's faithfulness? Not at all! Let God be true and every human be a liar.*" Even if we don't have faith, God is bigger and can override our lack of faith. God knows our heart intentions, even though our words and mind may not be in line. He is able to heal even if we hit the wall of unbelief.

Do you remember the story of Peter from Acts 12? An angel of God miraculously released him from prison during the night. He thought he was dreaming, but his experience was real. Peter quickly came to realize that this was better than a dream, he was out of jail! He walked to a house nearby, where he probably knew that an all night pray group would be meeting. He was excited at the prospect of seeing his friends face-to-face and sharing how God had delivered him.

Sure enough, when he got to the house, the people were deep in intercession, praying for his release. When the door was answered and the group was informed that it was Peter, those wonderful women and men of faith exhibited their lack of faith. They assumed the worst and thought it was his ghost at the door. God answered the prayers of those in the home even though they didn't believe what they were asking for. I'm so glad that this passage is in the Bible. There are so many times that I hit a wall with my faith. When it seems that the pain is more persistent than my faith, does that stop God? Not at all!

God is a healing God. Just like a leopard can't change his spots, so God cannot change (Jeremiah 13:23). That means that if God healed people in the past, he can still do it today! Remember, God is the one who does the healing. If you or I were doing the healing, we'd be stuck. The good news is that Father God is the one who does the healing through the anointing of the Holy Spirit. Our role is to partner with him. But make no doubt about it; God is the one doing the work.

Jesus got credit for doing miracles and healing the sick, even though he repeated that he was doing nothing. I've heard that Kathryn Kuhlman often said, "I don't take credit when people get healed, and I don't take credit when they don't." I'm not sure where she said it, but it's a great sentiment for all of us to keep in mind. Anyone who has an anointing for healing knows that there is a lot of pressure and expectation that comes to you as the "healer." If only they could get a "professional" like you to touch them, they would be healed. Regardless, our focus always needs to be on God and Holy Spirit. I've recently read Jamie Buckingham's biography of Kathryn Kuhlman, *Daughter of Destiny*. The book documents the many times she reminded people that she didn't heal anyone; she simply was the one who invited the Healer into the room.

For twelve years Catch The Fire Toronto hosted nightly meetings. At most of those meetings we had a guest speaker. One of the speakers that we had often was from Australia by the name of Al Furey. He had a special ability to believe for healing even when the circumstances said otherwise. At one of the Sunday night meetings, Al began to minister to a deaf man. The man told us that doctors had taken his eardrum out as a child as the result of a very bad flu. A rather drastic treatment, yet that was the procedure. Al proceeded to minister to the man. He didn't ask for the eardrum to be recreated; he prayed that the man would be able to hear. After a minute or so, Al began to snap his fingers and to everyone's astonishment the man could hear.

We had a woman on our prayer ministry team at that point who was a hearing specialist and had some tools of the trade with her. She took a look in his ear and said there was still no eardrum. It didn't matter—he was hearing! God is faithful to do what he wants to do.

Faith activates healing; your faith, my faith, and our friends' faith is important. But the heartbeat of God is for you to be healed and he is able to override any lack of faith. He is so much bigger than us. He has enough faith for the whole of creation.

DOUBT, THE ENEMY OF FAITH

Doubt is a killer. It stops faith from being activated and hinders what God wants to do. In Jesus' sermons about faith, he labeled doubt as an enemy several times.

> *"Have faith in God," Jesus answered. "Truly I tell you, if anyone says to this mountain, 'Go, throw yourself into the sea,' and does not doubt in their heart but believes that what they say will happen, it will be done for them. Therefore*

I tell you, whatever you ask for in prayer, believe that you have received it, and
it will be yours. MARK 11:22-24

Doubt begins to undermine the thoughts that God has already given us, to the point that we are no longer sure if they really came from him. After so much questioning we do nothing and nullify God's blessing. We stop what God wanted to do. Satan is a master at bringing doubt. It is one of his primary tools that he uses over and over again, because it works for him. When God spoke to Adam and Eve, Satan quickly stepped in with *"did God really say"* (Genesis 3:1).

When Jesus was in the desert learning his identity and destiny, Satan appeared and twice said to him, *"If you are the Son of God"* (Matthew 4:3,6). He was trying to plant doubt into the mind of Jesus, knowing that if he succeeded, Jesus' ministry would be handcuffed.

When Jesus went to his hometown he came face to face with doubt. These people, whom he had known since his childhood, were unable to believe that Jesus had anointing, authority to heal, or anything to give them. Their familiarity with his former life as a builder blinded them. Only a few healings took place in Nazareth that day. Mark 6:6 says, *"He [Jesus] was amazed at their lack of faith."* The people's doubt stopped Jesus from being able to minister to the full extent that God wanted.

Unfortunately, there are many times when I pray for people who talk themselves out of their healing. As I begin to interview them about their pain, they often share their stories—and their doubts. They don't mean to talk about their doubt, it just comes out in the words they use. I can remember ministering at a rural church where a friend of mine was pastoring. The church did not have a history of healings and was part of a denomination that didn't believe in signs and wonders. However, the pastor did believe, and over a few months had been getting his folks ready for this very meeting with me as the guest speaker. Wonderful healings were taking place. Every person our team touched and ministered to was being healed by the Lord. In the course of the evening, several people mentioned that there was a man downstairs who had left the meeting in severe pain.

It seemed odd to me that someone would have left the meeting to go and sit in another part of the building if they had come for healing, especially when great healings were taking place. The congregation was a very laid-back rural crowd where everyone knew each other. I asked for someone to go get him, and when they brought the man back, I interviewed him as I had done with everyone else. From the beginning of our conversation he verbalized doubt after doubt, not only in word but also in body language. I knew right away that although he said he wanted to be healed he really wasn't ready. He couldn't get himself to even begin to believe that his healing was possible. His doubt would have killed the meeting if I had let him continue talking. His pastor later agreed with me that while the man talked a good game, his thoughts and actions betrayed him. He was a man full of doubt with the potential to single-handedly strip all faith from the room. He didn't receive his healing, even though we tried to bring it to him.

CHANGING DOUBT TO FAITH

For those of us who minister healing on a regular basis, one of our roles is to bring faith in the room. We are to help doubters become doers. James tells us that we are to be doers of the word, not just hearers (James 1:22). Somehow, most of us let doubt overwhelm us and do nothing. Even if we know something is of God or we've had a God-thought, we often let Satan win by not acting on our revelation.

I believe the most effective way to build faith and erode doubt is doing something we all did in kindergarten, called show and tell. Jesus demonstrated great miracles and told people about the kingdom. Sometimes he talked first and then did miracles; sometimes it was the other way around. Telling stories is one way that we move people out of doubt. The gospel authors knew this and included story after story of Jesus healing people. Luke wrote the book of Acts with more stories than teachings. He knew that stories activate us to believe!

Storytelling is a great art. One of my favourite storytellers is Bill Prankard. He has preached at Catch The Fire Toronto more than any other guest speaker. In 1972, nearly six years after Bill started out in ministry, God began to use him to heal people in the Ottawa-area church where he was a pastor. He had picked up an anointing after attending a Kathryn Kuhlman meeting in the United States. Bill was contacted one day by a television program that followed a debate format. The guests were invited to present their positions and to bring audience members to support them. The program was live and aired across Canada.

The producers told Bill that the topic would be faith healing. A local mainline church minister would be on the opposite side of the debate. Would

Bill be willing to do the show? I think most of Bill's friends advised him not to, but he felt the Lord say to do the show. He chose people who had received healing to be in his portion of the audience. As people arrived, Bill saw an acquaintance, a local doctor, enter the studio. The doctor told Bill that "the other side" had invited him as part of their audience to give his medical opinion concerning faith healing. They had obviously assumed he would not believe in it.

The show went live and both sides presented their case. Bill shared how God heals. When the audience was invited to weigh in, the doctor stood and shocked the producers, the host, and the opposing side by declaring that he believed in miracles. He then pointed to a man in the audience and told them this man was one of his patients, and that he had been totally healed of terminal cancer in one of Bill's meetings. The doctor said he had all the tests and X-rays to prove that the cancer that had invaded almost every organ was now completely gone. The host then invited the patient to share his amazing story. The agenda of the producers and host was out the window. The program was full on for God and healing!

Did your spirit jump while you read this story? Your spirit was saying the amen that comes with knowing that what happened is truth, knowing that God loves to change the atmosphere, and knowing that God loves to do the impossible. For those of you who read the story and didn't jump, can I suggest that doubt may be overwhelming you? Take time to read the gospel accounts of Jesus again. Read through the book of Acts while reminding yourself that Jesus is the same yesterday, today, and tomorrow. Feed yourself on stories of the goodness of God and renew your mind.

DOUBT IS A CHOICE

Friends, doubt is the enemy of faith and goes contrary to everything that God wants. When you find yourself second-guessing and questioning the thoughts or impressions that come to you, recognize this as Satan seeking to plant those seeds of doubt. Choose to walk in the spirit of the first voice (God's) and not that of the second thought. Learn to recognize the voice of God; your Father speaks words of encouragement, life, and hope. Recognize that Satan speaks fear, doubt, and condemnation.

Your mind is not often your friend when it comes to the things of God. Paul, in Romans 12, says that your mind does not process properly on its own. It needs to be renewed. Paul was writing to believers; even we can't always trust our mind to guide us towards God. When I begin to realize that my mind is processing doubt, I try to shut it down as quickly as possible. I say, "Sorry Satan, but your thoughts have just confirmed to me that the first voice I heard was God, and I'm going to do the opposite of what you just said."

Use doubt as a weapon in your favour. Turn doubt into faith; make the choice to act rather than to back off. Honour the voice of God with instant obedience and you will see that God begins to honour you. You'll start to see healings and miracles happen. If you feel that doubt is a major issue in your life, I welcome you to pray the prayer of the father (from Mark 9:24) who knew that he had doubt:

> Father, I do believe; help me overcome my unbelief! Please take the "If you can?" out of my words, thoughts, and actions. Father I ask that you would help me to quickly accept your thoughts as my thoughts,

your words as my words, and that by believing I may have life. I ask
that doubt would begin to disappear from my life in the name of Jesus
Christ.

Let me pray for you:

I speak a release of faith into your spirit right now in the name of
Jesus Christ. I bless you to believe more in God's ability to heal than
in Satan's desire to steal your healing. Father, I ask in the name of
Jesus that your words and thoughts would so overwhelm my friend
with hope and life that they would have no recourse other than to
obey you. I bless them to hold on to the hope that you've put into their
spirit. I bless doubt to die and faith to increase. I thank you Father that
you care for each of us, and I commit my friend to you in the name of
Jesus. Amen!

CHAPTER 4

Lies That Steal My Healing

Lies are powerful things. They can stall progress. They can stop momentum. Until 1492, when Christopher Columbus sailed across the ocean blue, everyone thought the world was flat. They didn't even attempt to sail west! Why would they, if it meant facing a certain death?

Lies will steal your healing. If we believe what Satan says, we will miss what God wants to do for our health. I've already mentioned that one of the people who has greatly helped me in understanding healing is Roger Sapp. One of the most helpful talks I heard him give was on the topic of doubt. He addressed several lies that keep us from receiving our healing and I'd like to give my take on his thoughts.

At the beginning of this book I wrote about the struggle in the heavenly realms relating to our health. Jesus said that Satan comes to destroy our health, even to the point of premature death. Jesus came to oppose Satan and all of his works (John 10:10) through his death on the cross. Satan's fate has been sealed. So if Satan has been defeated, why do so many empower him by agreeing with his lies? The fact is, he is a master deceiver who knows that if he can get us to believe his lies, he is empowered him to activate negative things in our lives. His only power over us today is what we give him. Thankfully, we have authority in Jesus to break the power we handed over. So let's dive right in!

I'M NOT GOOD ENOUGH

One lie that countless individuals believe is "I'm not good enough." People may not say it directly, but I often hear it in statements such as "I know that God can heal but my life isn't the way it should be." Wrong, wrong, wrong! The whole basis of salvation is that we are not good enough. In and of ourselves we do not merit any favour from God. As for the process of sanctification, we can't change ourselves and become like Jesus without the supernatural work of God. The very same principle applies with our healing. When we try to be good (or think that we are not good enough), we become the issue. We block the flow of God's grace; in our pride we try to earn what has already been given. Healing is as much a free gift as reconciliation.

He went down with them and stood on a level place. A large crowd of his disciples was there and a great number of people from all over Judea, from

Jerusalem, and from the coastal region around Tyre and Sidon, who had come to hear him and to be healed of their diseases. Those troubled by impure spirits were cured, and the people all tried to touch him, because power was coming from him and healing them all. **LUKE 6:17-19**

I bet that some of the people in the crowd that day thought that they weren't good enough. In any crowd of people there are always those who are struggling with unworthiness. The good news is that what they thought made no difference to Jesus. He overrode their ungodly beliefs and healed them anyway. It didn't matter to Jesus whether the root of their sickness was a demonic attack, an accident, or anything else. He healed them all!

Our perceived unworthiness is not a valid reason for us to wait another day for our healing. Remember what Paul wrote in Romans 8:38-39:

For I am convinced that neither death nor life, neither angels nor demons, neither the present nor the future, nor any powers, neither height nor depth, nor anything else in all creation, will be able to separate us from the love of God that is in Christ Jesus our Lord.

If you've been believing that you are not good enough (and need to stay in your sickness until you are good enough), I encourage you to renounce that lie and receive your healing today. Nothing can separate us from the love of God. His desire is to minister health into our body now, not later on. We will never be good enough for God. We will never be able to earn our healing. Being good has no correlation with God's desire to heal us.

DRUG DEALER GETS SET FREE

Once, as I was ministering in Brazil, a young man came to speak with me. He said that he was a drug dealer. He was addicted to drugs and wanted to be free. With the help of a translator, we discussed the question in his heart—could God still accept him? My translator and I prayed that God would free him from addiction, and renounced the lie that he wasn't good enough.

My friend Gilberto Lima, a Brazilian who now leads a church in Toronto, was the speaker the next night while I was at a different church in the city. At the end of the night we exchanged stories back in our hotel room. Gilberto told me that a young man had given a testimony of receiving prayer the night before for his drug addiction. He told the people that the next day, while he was in his father's car, the Holy Spirit showed up. He was overwhelmed and laughed and laughed as the Holy Spirit came. He shared that he had been set free of drug addiction! Gilberto didn't know that he was the same man that I had ministered to the previous night. One of the keys for him receiving his healing was that he renounced the lie that God wouldn't receive him in his sin.

If you've been struggling with unworthiness, I'd like you to pray this prayer:

> *Father, I confess my sin of believing a lie. I have felt that somehow my healing is connected to my behaviour, my habits, and my lifestyle. I renounce this lie and acknowledge that my healing is not dependent on my being good, but rather on what Jesus has done for me, and the will of my Father. Holy Spirit come and minister your healing to me today. Thank you that you love us unconditionally! Amen.*

GOD IS WORKING ON MY CHARACTER

Of all the lies that we will look at, I hear this one the most. It sounds very godly, as do most lies, yet it empowers Satan to keep us from our healing. The essence of a lie is that it sounds godly. Satan is so insidious that his lies sound like truth; we tend to quickly receive them into our spirit.

Is there anyone alive who God is *not* working on? Not likely. God is involved in all of our lives, even those of us who are not yet followers of Jesus. If you are a Christian, your character is continuously being refined. That is part of the ministry of the Holy Spirit today. If our character, or lack of it, were keeping us from being healed, we would need to find answers to questions; at what level do we reach a maturity that allows for healing? When are we godly enough to satisfy a holy God?

Surely at least one person in the crowd that Jesus healed in Luke 6 had poor character traits. If our healing were conditional on character lessons, Jesus would not have been released to heal all. My guess is that most of those at this meeting with Jesus hadn't yet passed the character test. God doesn't wait for us to become like him, which is a very good thing! Imagine the physical conditions of the people listed in this passage. Some of these health issues were very severe. Many of them, as they saw Jesus, perhaps felt that their character was not up to par, but that did not stop them from getting healed.

HEALING FROM A WHEELCHAIR

A couple years ago we were having a goodbye reception for one of our pastoral couples that was leaving Catch The Fire to join another ministry. Duncan Smith, one of our pastors at the time (he and his wife Kate are now leading Catch The Fire Raleigh), was chatting to a woman from our congregation after the reception. Let me back up and tell you about Hillary. She had been involved in a car accident several years before that left her dependent on a wheelchair for accessibility. Hillary could stand for short periods of time, but to walk on her own was something she had not done in almost seven years. She had lost her job because of the injuries sustained. She loves Jesus and had many people pray for her healing.

Duncan asked Hillary if she had heard about the man who was healed out of a wheelchair the previous week. She had and was excited for him. When Duncan proceeded to ask Hillary when she was going to get out of her wheelchair, her answer was a form of this lie. She responded by saying that her character improvement was somehow linked to her healing. Duncan challenged her on this and encouraged her to repent, and she did. He then commanded her to stand up and walk. She pushed herself up out of the scooter. Then began to slowly walk. She walked faster and faster to the point that she was running around the church building.

Her twin sister Gillian and the few left in the building were amazed at the miracle that had just happened. Repenting of a lie was the key for Hillary's healing.

It gets better. Hillary's healing happened on a Sunday and early the next week she was due in court for the insurance settlement that had been postponed over and over again. The very week that she was to receive financial aid due to the negligence of the other driver she would be walking into the courtroom, healed. Naturally she was nervous that the judge would not give her the settlement she was looking for once he saw her walk. She went to court, testified as to what God did, and was awarded a settlement much larger than she anticipated. God is not only good; he is great!

I would like you to say this prayer and renounce the lie that your character affects your healing:

> *Father, forgive me for accepting this demonic lie into my spirit. I renounce it in all of its forms. I command any and all demonic spirits that were connected to this lie to stop their assignment. I command them to leave now in the mighty name of Jesus. Father, come now and fill me again with your Holy Spirit as you heal my body from every sickness and every bit of pain. In the name of Jesus, amen.*

PAUL'S THORN

Some people point to what the Bible says about Paul's thorn in his flesh. Wasn't Paul sick and God said he'd have to live with it? Here's a surprise: there is nothing in the passage to say that the thorn was a sickness or disease.

Take a look again at the passage in 2 Corinthians 12:7. It specifically says *"a messenger of Satan to torment me."* This sounds to me like a harassing demonic spirit rather than sickness. The word translated to *messenger* here is also translated to *angel* in other passages. Paul was saying a demonic angel, or evil spirit as we'd say, was tormenting him.

For years people have not read the text but listened to someone else's understanding of the text. Good and godly people who were misled have also misled us. If you read the whole passage you will see Paul writing about a number of his hardships. When Paul talked about weakness, he never included health issues, just the spiritual oppression that he was under as a pioneer and apostle in the work of Christ. Paul's thorn in the flesh had nothing to do with a sickness or pain.

GOD IS TEACHING ME A LESSON

"God can't heal me just yet because he is teaching me a lesson." Sounds good, but it is a lie. It doesn't line up with Scripture. The crazy part of this lie is that the person usually doesn't know what the lesson is they are supposed to be learning. They are on an endless hamster wheel, waiting for this magical day when they will wake up with the lesson learned and be healed.

Does God teach us lessons? Yes, every day. Life is a continuous learning experience. We learn about others, about God, and about ourselves. But lessons have nothing to do with our healing. Of course we will learn lessons along the journey of sickness, just as we are to learn lessons when we are in good health.

At sunset, the people brought to Jesus all who had various kinds of sickness, and laying his hands on each one, he healed them. Moreover, demons came out of many people, shouting, "You are the Son of God!" But he rebuked them and would not allow them to speak, because they knew he was the Messiah. LUKE 4:40–41

This passage is another one where everyone in a crowd was healed. If God can't heal those who are still learning lessons, then why was everyone in this crowd healed? Surely at least one person was learning a lesson! Surely all of them were learning lessons. I love this passage because it would appear to be the first recorded incident of multiple healings in the Gospels. Earlier in the day, Jesus had gone into a synagogue to teach. While he was there, a demon-possessed man interrupted the meeting. Jesus used the authority he had been given by his Father and told the demon to shut-up and get out (Mark 1:21–28).

The synagogue attendees were shocked and began to tell their friends what Jesus had done that morning. The people knew that Jesus had gone to Simon Peter's home; as soon as the Sabbath day ended at sundown, they brought their friends and family members who were sick and demonized. Because it was the Sabbath, no one could carry a stretcher with his or her brother on it. They had to wait several hours for the Sabbath to end. Imagine the anticipation as they waited for the last light to go down over the horizon.

Did Jesus stop to interview each person who came to ensure they were eligible for healing? Of course not. Surely there was at least one person in the crowd who was in the process of learning a lesson as a result of their sickness. If this lie were true, Jesus would not have healed *all*. The fact that all were healed proves that life lessons don't stop the healing process.

So why then do we disqualify ourselves? I've seen folks who are in severe pain and with destructive diseases pass up invitations for healing prayers. When I ask them why they didn't respond, I often hear them speak this lie to me. Because they believe the lie, they don't accept prayer. This is a demonic ploy from Satan. Most people believe that God can heal, but Satan has tricked some people into believe that they can't be healed yet.

CRUISE INTO HEALING

Sandra and I once enjoyed a thirteen-day cruise that took us from Florida, United States, into the Caribbean and then across the Atlantic Ocean to England. We spent a couple days with Phil and Gill Hunt who lead a church near Poole, England. Poole is a beautiful seaside town on the English Channel. It is home to some very expensive homes, private yachts, and nice restaurants.

One day, Phil and Gill took us to one of the nicer Italian restaurants. As we came in we were greeted by a very outgoing man. He was about 60, dressed smart, and wore designer glasses. He took us to our table, acted like we were his best friends, and hastily called the waiters over to begin to look after us. He did this for everyone else who came into the restaurant as well. I watched him while we were eating and noticed that he was walking with a limp.

Okay, I thought. *I'm going to do something about this!* At the end of the meal this man came over again to see how our evening was. I took the opportunity to ask him about is limp. Did he have a bad knee? No. What he had was a toe that had somehow positioned itself under the other toes. Walking was painful because he was stepping on his own toe. I asked him if he would like the pain to go. He looked at me as if I had just asked him if the Pope was Catholic. I explained that I helped to heal people and asked him say a simple prayer.

"But of course, if it will help me!" So we repeated my little prayer.

> *My healing belongs to me,*
> *because of what Jesus has done,*
> *I receive my healing now.*

I asked him to put pressure on his foot and as he did I was met with a look that I am used to: bewilderment. He took a few steps away from our table and then back with a very puzzled look on his face.

"Hallelujah!" he said out loud as he raised his hands in the air.

Lessons are not the key to receiving your healing. It is a gift of God, a part of God's will for everyone, everywhere. Let's deal with every issue that would hinder the will of God in our lives. God wants us healed, regardless of the life lessons we are learning. Friend, if you recognize that this lie is something you have believed, can I encourage you to pray the following?

> *Father, forgive me for accepting this lie into my life. I acknowledge*
> *that you are continuously teaching me lessons, but I confess that I*
> *have confused this with my lack of healing. I renounce this belief in all*
> *of its facets and command every demonic spirit that has enforced it*
> *to cease and desist. I command them to leave my body and I ask that*
> *the Spirit of God would come into my body and heal me.*

IT'S NOT GOD'S TIMING

Satan's lie about timing is usually tied to one of the other lies relating to being good enough and learning lessons. This lie is an attempt to have us put off our expectation for healing to another day. This lie is in absolute contradiction to what Jesus said to Zacchaeus in Luke 19:9: "*Today salvation [sozo] has come to this house.*"

Hebrews 3 and 4 are full of passages that basically say that today is the day of salvation. God is never asking that we postpone anything to tomorrow, other than anxiety. Many of you will know that the Greek word *sozo* can be translated as salvation, healing, or deliverance. These words are used interchangeably. God never wants anyone to wait for their healing. Satan, on the other hand, loves for people to postpone the things God wants to do for us today. God is always about today.

Can you remember the process of when you became a follower of Jesus? If you were like me, you had felt the convicting promptings of the Holy Spirit often. I kept postponing God's invitation for many months. I put off what God wanted to do. Did God want me to wait to get saved or did Satan?

> *When Jesus heard what had happened, he withdrew by boat privately to a solitary place. Hearing of this, the crowds followed him on foot from the towns. When Jesus landed and saw a large crowd, he had compassion on them and healed their sick.* MATTHEW 14:13-14

I'm going to use the same point I've used with the other lies. Following the logic of this lie, in this crowd of thousands we would expect at least one person was out of God's timing and not meant to be healed that day. Again, Jesus didn't interview the crowd to make sure it was alright to heal them on that day. Every person who came into the presence of Jesus and requested healing was healed. Delaying a healing never entered his mind. In fact, you won't find Jesus praying and asking Father God if he should minister to people. He automatically assumed that every person he met should be healed right then and there, no questions asked.

There is only one passage in the Scriptures that even remotely seems to say that God waits to heal. This is the story of the man born blind from John 9. You'll remember that the disciples were wondering who had sinned and caused him to be born blind. Jesus' response was sharp and to the point: *"This happened so that the work of God might be displayed in him. As long as it is* day, *we must do the work of him who sent me. Night is coming, when no one can work,"* (John 9:3-4, emphasis added).

One of the subtleties that Gentiles miss when reading Bible stories is how days start and end for the Jews. A day finishes when night comes. The Jewish Sabbath begins and ends at dusk. Do you see the point Jesus is making? Today or *day* is when Jesus wanted to minister. Jesus was telling his disciple not to worry about what had happened in the past, but to focus on what God wanted for that day. Jesus did not want to postpone anyone's healing to the next day, or what he called *night*.

Healing is a massive priority for Father God and Jesus knew that. He healed everyone who wanted ministry every time. No thought of timing, ever. This is a powerful truth for us. Please don't let anyone talk you out of seeking your healing. Please don't believe the lies of Satan that say this is not your time. If Satan says "later," that should be proof to you that God wants it today; Satan always opposes the things of God.

HEALING IN BANGLADESH

Terry Bone is one of my friends. We got touched by the Holy Spirit about the same time at the revival meetings in Toronto. I came from the Baptist tradition and he from the Pentecostal. Somehow our timing connected us. Terry used to pastor a great Holy Spirit church west of Toronto. He then moved to a teaching and training role and somehow came across a group of churches in Bangladesh led by a banker. I've been to Bangladesh twice with him, each time training their leaders on how to minister healing.

On my last trip a Muslim friend of mine joined me. Joe, whose real name is Mohammed, owns a restaurant near our church. I've known him for years, first as a waiter, and now as the owner of a Greek restaurant. Joe has received healing from me, and now as the owner, insists that I pray for his staff whenever I'm there. He asked to join Terry and I on the trip. On my last day in his country, Joe took me to meet some of his family and friends. I won't go into the entire story, as there are security implications. I found myself in the home of a wealthy businessman. His sister and her two teenage sons were living with them while their dad was seeking refugee status in Canada.

As we were eating Joe told the family how I have impacted the husband in Canada. They were very thankful for my involvement and were treating me like a hero. At one point I heard the Holy Spirit tell me that the lady was sick. I asked her if she had pain, only to find out that she had just gotten out of bed because she had been suffering with a fever for four days.

When I asked if I could pray for her, the older of her two sons objected. I don't know if it was because I was a Christian, or if it was their holy day, or something else, but he didn't want me to minister. Joe stepped in and told the family that every time I pray for people they are healed. He told of the times I had successfully prayed for the husband in Canada. They finally consented.

I had her say the little prayer that I have used around the world. When I asked her how she was, they all stared at her except for Joe. Without glancing up from his Blackberry he stated, "She's better, isn't she?" And she was. She was completely free of fever. The family subsequently all said a prayer to invite Jesus into their lives. I didn't have the option of waiting for a later time for her. I was leaving that night to return to Canada. God wanted her healed right then, not at a later time, which may not have come.

If you have ever thought about timing, you aren't alone. Most people I know have the same lingering questions. When your mind embraces what the Bible teaches, that God wants you healed today, healing begins to happen. When you doubt what the Bible teaches, you postpone your healing to sometime in the future. Sadly, many never get around to "that" day.

What will you believe today? If you know that this lie has been a part of your past, or is still part of your present, I encourage you to renounce it immediately. Agree with me by saying this prayer:

er, I understand that I have sinned by believing my healing was for another day. I see that I have accepted a lie and I repent of it now. I renounce this lie and all its effects. I choose for you to heal me today. I deserve my healing because of Jesus' death and I receive my healing now. Please renew my mind. Strip my mind from all lies that would delay my healing. Thank you for your healing works in my life. In the name of Jesus, amen.

SICKNESS IS HOW WE DIE

Some believe that sickness is acceptable because sooner or later we all have to die. How else are we going to die if sickness doesn't decay our bodies? Well-meaning people convince themselves and others that their sickness will stay with them until they die. They throw their hands up in the air and say, "God's will be accomplished. I'm destined to live a life of pain and suffering until I die." Yes, people talk a lot along these lines, but they have believed a lie that ultimately may lead them to die prematurely. Muslims and Hindus believe this theory, but it is not a Christian truth.

Jesus left there and went along the Sea of Galilee. Then he went up on a mountainside and sat down. Great crowds came to him, bringing the lame, the blind, the crippled, the mute and many others, and laid them at his feet; and he healed them. The people were amazed when they saw the mute speaking, the crippled made well, the lame walking and the blind seeing. And they praised the God of Israel. MATTHEW 15:29-31

This passage is very similar to the ones we've read featuring a large crowd and a significant miracle. In the previous one, the miracle was the feeding of 5,000 men, this time Jesus was feeding at least 3,000 people. The point of the story is incredible. Severely sick people—the blind, the crippled, the deaf and dumb—were all healed. My assumption is that less serious diseases were also healed. Once again there is no record of Jesus asking God's permission to heal the sick. He simply sees the needs of the people and, knowing the Father's will, heals everyone. I love it!

If sickness were a way for God to end our days, then Jesus violated God's will on that day. And not just on that day, but repeatedly. Surely, Jesus should have asked the Father who from the crowd was supposed to die. But that isn't what happens. Jesus ministers to everyone who has need, and this passage specifically mentions extreme physical issues.

Remember what we talked about in the first chapter? God is opposed to every work of Satan. Satan is the author of sickness and disease. Jesus never thought twice about healing people because he knew that his Father wanted them to be healthy. One of my regrets is not knowing this earlier. In 1985, my father died from a cancer that had taken over most of the organs of his body. My family, who were all believers, never laid hands on my dad and asked God to heal him. We had been taught, among other lies, that it was presumptuous to ask God to heal someone; it was inappropriate of us "mere mortals." So our family did pray and ask God to heal my dad, but we did that in our own times of prayer. We didn't minister my dad by the laying on of hands, as the Bible teaches Jesus did. We didn't pray the prayer of faith that James tells us to. We had bought into a series of lies that stopped us from acting.

HOW ARE WE SUPPOSED TO DIE?

From what I see in the Bible, God wants us to die of old age, not because of some sickness. He certainly doesn't want us going out in terrible pain. Where is the glory in dying that way? Where is the testimony of a loving God in that? I love the stories about the patriarchs in Genesis. Do you remember how Abraham, Isaac, and Jacob died? They each lived a long healthy life without any instances of sickness recorded. They knew when they were about to die, so they gathered their children close to them, blessed them, and then went to be with the Lord. That is how I want to die. Old and healthy, with my wife Sandra, my children, grandchildren, and great-grandchildren around my bed and a smile on my face!

Keith is one of the men at our church who came to know the Lord in his retirement years. Right after Keith gave his life to Jesus, he was in Florida, where he had family, and heard of an elderly relative that was in a coma at the hospital. She was not expected to live. The family decided that because she was old and close to death they would begin to settle her estate while she was still living. They emptied her house, sold her furniture, and got rid of her clothes. Well I guess Keith didn't know this was happening. Because he was a new Christian, Keith didn't know that people are "supposed" to die of sickness. All he knew was that Jesus heals, so off he went to the hospital to minister to the lady. I think you can guess the rest of the story. Keith's prayer worked and she was revived. Revived and not very happy at her relatives when she found out what they had done. They believed that her sickness would lead to her death. Keith believed otherwise.

Friends, do not accept sickness into your body! Do not believe that the pain you have will be with you for the rest of your life! Do not believe that the sickness you have will lead or contribute to your death! If you do, you have believed a lie and accepted a curse; you have invited Satan to have access to your life. Jesus showed us time and time again that God's heart is for everyone, everywhere, to be healed! Please repeat this prayer to break this lie:

> *Father, forgive me for partnering with Satan in this lie. I confess that I have believed a lie and allowed it to enter my mind, my body, and spirit. I renounce this lie and its curse over my body. I send it back to hell, where it came from, in the powerful name of Jesus. I ask that you would take this pain out of my body and eradicate all my diseases today. In the name of Jesus I pray.*

BUT I DON'T BELIEVE IN JESUS!

The question often comes up, "Can I get healed if I don't believe in Jesus?" The answer is a resounding yes! There are many stories of unbelievers receiving miraculous healings. Take a look at John 9, where Jesus ministered healing to a man who was born blind. He had not yet recognized Jesus when he was healed—it appears from the story that Jesus does not declare his identity until after the healing.

> *Jesus heard that they had thrown him out, and when he found him, he said, "Do you believe in the Son of Man?"*
> *"Who is he, sir?" the man asked. "Tell me so that I may believe in him."*
> *Jesus said, "You have now seen him; in fact, he is the one speaking with you."*
> *Then the man said, "Lord, I believe," and he worshiped him.* JOHN 9:35-38

Jesus spit into some dirt, made mud, and put it on the man's eyes. He then told the man to go and wash his face. Jesus was not with the young man when his eyesight was restored. When he washed his face, his blind eyes miraculously opened and he could see, but he still had no idea who it was that healed him. The miracle causes such a disturbance that the previously-blind man and his parents were brought to the Jewish leaders to explain what had happened. The parents were willing to testify that their son was blind but now could see.

While their son was being questioned, it came out that it was Jesus who had put the mud on his face. This man did not even know what Jesus looked like. When they did meet again later in the day, Jesus introduced himself. The response of the man was "Lord, I believe," instantly affirming his belief in the Son of God.

This is even more evidence that God wants everyone healed. God is a healing God who does not discriminate—he doesn't care what disease you have, what nationality you are, whether you are his follower or not. He heals simply because he loves you and doesn't want you ill or in pain.

HEADS OR TAILS?

I raised both of my sons to be athletes. Both played baseball at the top level as they were growing up. Most of the same kids made the team year after year, so the parents got to know each other well. There are only so many topics to discuss when you are sitting in the bleachers watching your sons play; most parents knew that I was a pastor.

Once, my oldest son Jon was playing in a tournament and our team ended the round robin with an identical record as another team. It was all down to a coin toss, determining who would move on to the semi-finals and who would go home. Our team got to pick either heads or tails. The coach, who was not a follower of Jesus but obviously a wise man, decided that if anyone could hear from God on this important decision, it would be the "preacher." So the coaches all came to me along with the other parents and explained the situation. "Is it going to be heads or tails?" This would be an important moment in my life and for my reputation as a Christian. I prayed quickly, got an answer and picked tails. They triumphantly marched to the tournament officials for the coin toss. I joined them, continuing to intercede while trying to look confident. Tails it was! The men all wanted to buy me a beer to celebrate our victory. As it turned out, our team won the tournament!

Besides showing me in a good light, the experience opened doors for me with the other parents. A Hindu grandparent came to me at one of the subsequent baseball games asking for prayer for sickness. I asked why he wanted me to pray for him. His answer was very interesting: "because Jesus heals the sick!" It seems that even those who don't have a personal relationship with Jesus know that he heals sick people. Almost every sick person I've prayed for who isn't yet a follower of Jesus has been healed.

For some reason, followers of Jesus seem to have more hang-ups about healing than do those who have not yet embraced a relationship with him. Believing in Jesus as your Saviour is not a prerequisite to being healed. In fact, it would appear that many people were healed by Jesus before he explained who he was. I want to encourage you to believe what God says about healing: "I am the Lord who heals you" (Exodus 15:26).

The question I have for you today is this: Are you willing to do what the blind man did after he was healed? Are you willing to believe that Jesus is your Lord? When the healed man understood that it was Jesus who had performed the miracle, he began to put things together. Perhaps he understood that no one in the Old Testament had ever been healed of blindness (and that for Jesus to heal him was a big deal). Probably not. But, he knew Jesus was someone special. When they met again, he instantly began to worship Jesus and acknowledge his supremacy by calling him Lord.

I would love to pray two prayers for you today. The first is for your healing and the second is for you to acknowledge Jesus as your Lord. Will you pray these prayers with me?

> *Father, I thank you that my friend recognizes they have a need for healing. I thank you that you alone are our healer. Father, come right now and touch my friend's body and bring them their healing. Heal my friend just like you healed the blind man many years ago. In the name of Jesus, amen.*

Now is your opportunity to respond back to him:

> *Father, I choose to believe that Jesus Christ is your Son and that he came and lived on earth to represent you. I believe what the Bible says, that he died on a cross for my sins and three days later was raised to life. His resurrection proves that my sins, which have separated me*

from you, have been dealt with. Now I am forgiven. Jesus, please come into my life and be my Lord! Amen!

If you prayed this last prayer and meant it, the Bible says that you are now a follower of Jesus. The Holy Spirit of God has now taken up residence in your life and will be with you forever. His role is to help you follow after God and he will begin to show you your true identity and destiny. For those of you who prayed this prayer, would you send me an email (stevelong@ catchthefire.com)? I have some resources that I'd love to send you free of charge to help you develop your relationship with Jesus. May God bless you in every area of your life!

CHAPTER 5

Jesus Never Healed Anyone

Let's start this chapter with a life changing revelation: Jesus did not heal a single person.

> The centurion replied, "Lord, I do not deserve to have you come under my roof. But just say the word, and my servant will be healed. For I myself am a man under authority, with soldiers under me. I tell this one, 'Go,' and he goes; and that one, 'Come,' and he comes. I say to my servant, 'Do this,' and he does it." When Jesus heard this, he was amazed and said to those following him, "Truly I tell you, I have not found anyone in Israel with such great faith. I say to you that many will come from the east and the west, and will take their places at the feast with Abraham, Isaac and Jacob in the kingdom of heaven. But the subjects of the kingdom will be thrown outside, into the darkness, where there will be weeping and gnashing of teeth." Then Jesus said to the centurion, "Go!

Let it be done just as you believed it would." And his servant was healed at that moment. MATTHEW 8:8-13

The passage listed above is an incredible one. In terms of how Jesus ministered healing, it is one of the most profound sections of Scripture in the whole Bible. The most important revelation that I've had in the past few years is wrapped up in it; Jesus, while he lived on planet earth, did nothing of himself. Every person Jesus met was healed not because of Jesus' divinity but because God wanted them healed. They were healed through the anointing of the Holy Spirit that Jesus carried. Jesus was simply the conduit for the healing. He was the one who spoke the words, laid on hands, rebuked diseases and demons, but he didn't heal people by his own power or authority.

This nameless centurion was the first person to figure this out. It took a man who was used to authority and knew the principle of chain of command to see what was really happening. Because of his military training, the centurion got it. Despite Jesus trying over and over to tell his Twelve, as well as the multitudes, that he was only doing the will of his Father, everyone kept thinking that Jesus was the healer.

But the centurion saw that Jesus was under authority and knew how delegated authority worked. A commander tells a lower ranking officer what his or her desire is, and then that officer passes on the orders to those beneath him. Eventually a task is accomplished by a lower ranking person. This centurion begins by making a shocking statement: *"But just say the word, and my servant will be healed. For I myself am a man under authority,"* (vv. 8-9). What he was essentially saying was "Jesus, you are just like me, not giving the orders but rather carrying them out on behalf of someone else."

When this concept really hit home with me, my healing ministry improved dramatically. Jesus didn't heal people because he was God (even though he *was* God); he healed people because God ordered him to do so. So when I minister, it is not up to me whether a person is healed. My role is simply to be under authority and do what I've had revelation to do!

The powerful story of the hemorrhaging woman also demonstrates this. We saw in chapter 3 that this lady had been bleeding for twelve years. She had been to all the doctors, she had spent all her money, and no one was able to help her. One encounter with Jesus and she was healed, right?

Well, sort of. She was healed when she touched Jesus but Jesus didn't heal her. In fact, Jesus was not even aware that he was taking part in a miraculous healing. He had no idea that in this crowd of people pushing, straining to touch him, one lady was touching him with a purpose. While others were looking for an autograph, she was looking for a healing. This lady knew in her spirit, because of a revelation from Father God, that if she touched Jesus she could be healed. So she came out of a place of seclusion and headed into a crowd. In doing so, she broke the ceremonial codes of law from Leviticus relating to women's menstruation. She stepped into the crowd and did what God had whispered to her.

Jesus was quickly able to discern that this was no ordinary touch. How? We often miss key parts of a story, so don't miss this one: Jesus felt the anointing of God flow through his body. Because he felt power leaving him, he knew that someone had been healed. But up until that moment, he was oblivious of what was about to happen. I used to think that Jesus tapped into his divine abilities while he ministered on planet earth, but this passage shows the opposite. If Jesus was actively living in his divine nature, and not that of a man, he would have known that this lady was approaching him, and would have even been able to spot her in the crowd instead of waiting for her to reveal herself.

Jesus did not heal this lady through his own divinity. If he had done so, he would have modeled an unattainable ministry. We aren't divine; how in the world would we be able to minister like Jesus did if he was functioning as God? There would be no possible way for us to match him, let alone do the "greater things" that he talked about in John 14:12.

If God wants someone well, and I believe the Scriptures teaches that he does, it is his responsibility to do it. However, God loves to use people like us to restore health to another person. He involves people in doing his bidding. There are no stories in the Scriptures, which I can recall, of God healing people without using a human being. To the best of my knowledge, God always partners with a person like Paul or Peter (or Jesus!) to see someone healed. Jesus had no advantage over us when it came to healing. In and of himself, Jesus never healed one person. The servant was healed because of the faith of the centurion. All Jesus did was respond to the man's faith with an affirmation and with a word: "Go!"

Whether you are a novice or a seasoned minister of healing, this principle is key. You and I don't heal people. God does it every time, no exceptions. But we all get to partner in seeing healing come to others!

FIFTY CANCER HEALINGS

In 2006, one of my friends, Jack Frost, died. He had battled lung cancer; he
visited many specialists and did all the right things in pursuit of healing. I
don't know why, but the Lord received Jack into glory rather than heal his
body on earth. He had ministered at our church numerous times. He was a
powerful teacher and minister in the topic of God's extravagant love for us.

On the Sunday morning that we got the news that Jack was not well and
may pass into eternity at any moment, our church prayed for him like many
other groups of believers. Sandra and I were on a plane that night to the
United Kingdom to minister. Both of us were woken from our sleep on the
plane at the same time. We looked at each other and in our spirits we both
knew that Jack had just died. I can remember us quietly crying on the plane
while everyone else was sleeping.

As I was thanking the Lord for Jack and saying a prayer for his three children and his wife, Trish, the Lord spoke something to me. He said that as
punishment for Satan prematurely taking Jack's life that I would see 50
people healed of cancer that year. Wow. I told Sandra what I had heard
and pondered what that would look like.

Our first meeting was in the Liverpool area the following night. There
was no time to really get over jet lag. We jumped into a meeting right
away. Kevin Peat, a great friend of ours and leader in the Elim Pentecostal
churches in the United Kingdom, was our host. At the end of the meeting
we had a time to pray for those who were battling sickness and disease.
At one point in the ministry time, a woman introduced her father to me.
He was dying of bile duct cancer. The toxins in his body could not be

released and his skin was yellow. I remember that he was in a wheelchair and breathing via oxygen.

I had the Lord's promise to me, not even twelve hours earlier, that cancer would be healed as a tribute to my friend Jack Frost. I didn't feel anything special, I simply prayed as I would for any other person. Nothing noticeably happened other than the man had less pain. He was still yellow, still in a wheelchair, and still using oxygen when he left the meeting that night. Something happened though. I got an email within a few days from the daughter. She wrote to tell me that her dad was still pain-free by the time they got home from the meeting. When he woke up the next morning he still had no pain. Not only that, but he was feeling strength in his body. Not only that, but his body wasn't yellow anymore! He went to the doctors several times in the next weeks. He had every test possible, because the doctors were dumbfounded as to how this could have happened. Each test came back saying that he no longer had cancer. He was healed!

I ended up losing count of the cancer healings that year, but there were many, and I certainly prayed for hundreds of people. I believe God delivered fully on his promised punishment of Satan, and will continue to do so!

IN HIS OWN WORDS

Jesus himself confirmed the miraculous healings taking place were not by his hand, when he said, "*I do nothing on my own but speak just what the Father has taught me*" (John 8:28-29). He repeated this sentiment often:

For I did not speak on my own, but the Father who sent me commanded me to say all that I have spoken. I know that his command leads to eternal life. So whatever I say is just what the Father has told me to say. JOHN 12:49–50

Because of the anointing on his life, Jesus began to see crowds of people coming to him for healing. They pleaded with him for a touch, for a prayer. Many had begun to believe that Jesus was the Messiah. Attention was heaped on him, and he tried to deflect it. Jesus must have known that they thought that he was the miracle worker. Seven times in John's gospel, Jesus told people that he was simply the middleman, getting revelation from the Father and then obeying it. That obedience was the reason miracles and healings were taking place. It wasn't him, but him serving a loving Father.

In John 5, Jesus says it again in response to accusations of Sabbath violation from the Jewish leaders: *"By myself I can do nothing; I judge only as I hear, and my judgment is just, for I seek not to please myself but Him who sent me"* (John 5:30). Jesus had just healed the lame man who could not get into the pool near the Sheep Gate in Jerusalem. Earlier, verse 16 says that because this healing happened on a Sabbath, the Jews began to persecute Jesus.

Let me paraphrase his simple defense: Yes I know this is the Sabbath, and yes I know you have lots of regulations about what you believe is correct, but I only do what I hear my Father asking me to do. My Father asked me to minister to this man today and so I obeyed. If you have a problem, take it up with him!

Friends, if only our lives were that simple. If we could live each and every day only doing what Father God speaks to us, our lives would be so very different. Can you begin to imagine what kind of ministry God would trust you with if he knew that every word he spoke to you would be obeyed?

You may be better than me at this, but I know that there are many times when I hear God perfectly well. The problem is that I also listen to Satan's voice. His voice leads me to fear and to rationalize away what I heard; his doubts too often cancel what God said. When Satan gets in the way, I often hesitate and give in rather than obey my Father.

I can remember a time several years ago when I was waiting in a hotel by our church building for Kevin and Margaret Peat. They were coming to our home for lunch. As I was sitting in the lobby waiting, I began to look around and watch people. My eye was drawn to a gentleman in the souvenir shop. I distinctly remember hearing God say, *The man is sick, go and pray for him.* I looked around the lobby of the hotel to see if anyone else had heard this voice and after it looked like no one had, I reluctantly decided it was meant for me rather than the general public. Back then I wasn't great at beginning conversations with strangers (I've since gotten better). I was hoping someone else would respond and look after this man, but alas, God was only speaking to me.

I got up and went into the shop. No one was there other than this shopkeeper at the counter. I was trying to think how to best approach him and decided that if I had something in my hand it would work better. So, I grabbed a Diet Coke from the cooler and walked to the counter.

When I got there I said to the man, "By any chance are you not feeling well today?" He responded back that indeed he was sick. Wow! God was right. Now what do I do?

I said to the man, "Sir, I'm a follower of Jesus and I was just sitting in the chairs over there when I felt God saying that you were sick and to come and heal you. Can I pray for you?" He glanced around awkwardly to see who was watching. We were still alone so he agreed. Because he didn't close his eyes for the prayer, neither did I. I looked at him and began to pray. As soon as I said the word *Father*, God spoke again. He told me that this man had the flu, so I included that in my prayer: "Father, I ask that right now that you would take away the flu that this man is experiencing in Jesus' name, Amen."

I then did another awkward thing for me. I asked the manager to take a deep breath and let me know how he felt. He took a deep breath and said he was absolutely fine. Wow, that was fast! I was a bit shocked at how quick he was healed. I then heard him say these profound words:

"That will be a dollar please."

I still hadn't paid for my Diet Coke.

PAUL'S REVELATION

The point I'm trying to make is that Jesus did not heal people in and of himself. He was entirely dependent on God for authority and power, as well as for the revelation of whom to minister to. Perhaps the clearest passage to show this is this segment from Philippians 2:6-8:

> *[Jesus] Who, being in very nature God,*
> *did not consider equality with God something to be used to his own advantage;*
> *rather, he made himself nothing*
> *by taking the very nature of a servant,*
> *being made in human likeness.*
> *And being found in appearance as a man,*
> *he humbled himself*
> *by becoming obedient to death—*
> *even death on a cross!*

A couple key points need to be made so that there is no confusion. First, the apostle Paul clearly tells us that Jesus is God in his choice of words: *"who being in very nature God."* Second, Paul also says that Jesus made a choice to not function in his divine attributes. Not only was Jesus God, but he also had all the strengths and abilities of God. Jesus is, was, and will always be God.

As God, Jesus made a world-changing choice. He chose to humble himself as low as he could go. Jesus, who was in his very nature God, decided not to hold on to that status. He made himself nothing! He voluntarily gave up all his rightful God-attributes in order to be a substitute for us on the cross. I have known this truth for years, but I didn't understand the implications for a healing ministry. I've grown up with a stronger sense of the divinity of Jesus than of his humanity. Because of that mindset, I've always seen the miracles, the healings, the insights into the thoughts of people, as something that only the divine Son of God could do. I never thought that others could function like this, certainly not me.

However, this passage says that Jesus *"made himself nothing."* The root of this phrase is to make empty or to neutralize something. Jesus gave up the privileges of divinity even though they were rightfully his, not only so that he could stand in our place when it came to the cross, but also to show us how to live and minister in the spirit realm.

Jesus did not have an unfair advantage over us. He lived each day, as it were, in our shoes. Unlike us though, he never once sinned. He never contaminated his relationship with God. Despite all the temptations, despite all the trials and tests, despite Satan himself, Jesus always chose to listen to and obey his Father. Most of us sin daily and because of that we struggle in the process of representing God. There is the hope for us. We too can choose to obey the voice of our Father and we too can do the greater things that Jesus talked about.

OBEDIENCE IS KEY TO HEALING THE SICK

So, if Jesus did not have an advantage over you and me, how did he do the healings and miracles? In a word, obedience. He always did what his Father spoke to him. He always did what his Father showed him. He responded to his Father in every situation exactly as Father wanted him to.

When you and I get to that stage we will begin to see the same results that Jesus did. There is a popular statement that says, "if you always do what you've always done; you'll always get what you've always got." Jesus always got God's intended results because he always obeyed and did what the Father directed him to do. If we change from doing what is right some of the time to doing it all the time, we'll definitely see a change in our ministries.

This is our challenge. This is my challenge. Learning to die to myself and to fully rely on God. Friends, the quicker we learn this lesson, the quicker we'll grow and mature in the things of God. Obedience is something we train our children for from their earliest years. Obedience is what is drilled into every military enlister, to the point that they absolutely trust a senior officer. When we learn to obey every order from Father, we will see the greater miracles in our ministries.

One of my personal struggles in having a healing ministry is not trying to figure everything out. I come from a tradition in church where truth has to make sense. My ancestors are British, which means that logic is foundational to everything I do. I wasn't brought up to trust intuition. Jesus, living completely as a human, had to develop his intuitive side. He had to learn to listen to the Father. He had to learn to value thoughts, ideas, visions, pictures, feelings, etc. He also got very good at it! Christians and unbelievers are also wired for this.

I was once in Edinburgh, Scotland, having breakfast with Pastor Richard Iredale. We had two ladies looking after us as we sampled the buffet. The older woman was bubbly and full of life. I asked her if she had pain in her body and she responded with a yes. But she didn't want me to do anything to help her.

The younger woman overheard me telling Richard a story about healing. She lingered at the table and I asked her if she'd like to hear the rest of the story. That led to a fifteen-minute conversation about God. She began to share some of her story and told me that she gets premonitions. Her fiancé thought she was crazy, as did others. For us as pastors to validate her and say that God was talking to her was life giving. She promised to come to Richard's church in Broxburn and find out more.

JOHN'S REVELATION

John was the writer of the fourth biography of the life of Jesus. He would most likely have read the accounts from Matthew, Mark, and Luke. Most of his record of Jesus is new material, as there was no need for him to say things that had already been written.

He begins his narrative with a quick overview. He takes us to the very beginning of time in verse 14 and tells us that *"the Word became flesh and made his dwelling among us."* In the first verse he also states that *"the Word was God."* By verse 10 John has skipped to Jesus' relative John the Baptist, who would introduce Jesus to the world stage. John, the apostle, tells us that although Jesus made the world, his purpose in coming to earth was to take us to the Father so we could *"become children of God"* (John 1:12).

John clearly tells us that Jesus was and is divine. But John also knew that there was a humanity to Jesus that his readers needed to recognize right up front, in the first chapter of his biography. Both John and Paul wanted to make this point that Jesus, though God, did not do miracles and healings using his divine powers.

John was a late bloomer as an author. He didn't write his account of Jesus' life until Matthew, Mark, and Luke have already been published. His account is very distinct: because the other gospels were in print (so to speak), his story fills in gaps and is more of an overview rather than a chronological story. In his writings, John uses the number 7 constantly, which is the number of perfection in the Bible.

Jesus was the perfect healer; he tells seven stories of healings.
Jesus was the perfect teacher; there are seven sermons.
Jesus was the perfect representative of God; he gave seven *I am* statements.
Jesus was the perfect follower; there are seven times when John records that Jesus only did what he saw or heard.

John wanted everyone to know that Jesus was absolutely divine. He was God. He was eternal, living before the creation of the world. In fact, Jesus helped in creation. But John also clearly wanted his readers to know that while there was divine perfection, there was also Jesus the human being. John states that Jesus *"became flesh."* He not only took our form, but also dwelt among us with all the imperfections of our frail bodies. He became the God-man. John wanted us to understand that Jesus lived like us, and was still perfect.

What was John referring to in verse 14 when he says, *"We have seen his glory, the glory of the one and only Son"*? *Glory* is a word that John uses more than any other gospel authors. When John uses this word, I believe he is talking about seeing what God wants us to see. Let me explain: in John 2 there is the story of Jesus turning the water to wine. John concludes the narrative in verse 11 by saying that Jesus *"thus revealed his glory."*

In John 11, when Lazarus is raised from the dead, Jesus talks to Martha and says, *"Did I not tell you that if you believed, you would see the glory of God?"* For Jesus, *Glory* was doing what God wanted in the face of doubt, unbelief, and ignorance. Even as a man, Jesus knew what his Father wanted and did it every time. Glory came as a result. People began to put their faith in Jesus because of the miracles and healings. Jesus embodied obedience to God's desire and will. What is it then that John wants us to understand right from the beginning of his narrative about Jesus?

It is this: Jesus, though he was God, was also fully man. He always represented his Father. He did nothing on his own, only what his Father showed or spoke to him. By doing and saying what God wanted, he brought glory to those around him.

John knew that every healing and miracle was not done by Jesus the divine, but rather Jesus the man acting as a reflection of who God was. This leads me to then ask the obvious question: Am I doing the same? Am I always doing what God wants? Do I bring God's glory to the people around me so they can get a sense of how awesome God is?

Friends, this is our mission when it comes to a healing ministry. We are to let people see God through our actions. We are to do his stuff on earth to the extent that people are awestruck and have no choice but to glorify God. Remember, signs and wonders are part of what we are expected to do as we emulate the ministry of Jesus. The signs point the way to God. The wonders cause people to gasp and think *how did that happen?*

MIRACLE IN INDIA

James Maloney was recently at our church and was teaching in our School of Ministry. He told us the story that took place when he was in India in the early days of his ministry. He was leading a large, crusade-style meeting. He and his team would heal the sick and as a result people would turn from their Hindu or Muslim tradition and become followers of Jesus.

A man who had a hand but no arm was brought to the stage for ministry. One of his hands was attached directly to the shoulder. James prayed and nothing happened. Then he had a thought to get one of his intercessors to minister.

The Lord prompted him to a lady who hadn't wanted to minister to anyone; she simply wanted to be an intercessor. James told us that when she put her hand on the man's hand and began to pray, an arm shot out from the shoulder and began to flap around. He said it took two days for the man to gain control of the arm. Wow! What would that miracle say to someone in the crowd who was wondering if Jesus was real? You can bet that many came to know Jesus as Saviour that day.

The apostle John taught us that Jesus the man was the perfect representative of God. Jesus the one who is just like you and me. We are to reflect what God wants to a world that doesn't know or grasp how wonderful he is. The reason I'm hitting at this point is simply this: you and I can do everything that Jesus did.

If Jesus always relied on Father for his directions, we can do that.
If Jesus always relied on Father for his anointing, we can do that.
If Jesus always relied on Father for his power and authority, we can do that.

I've had several theological breakthroughs in my Christian journey in the area of healing. Each of them moves me to a higher level of confidence in ministering to the sick. There is nothing that Jesus did that you and I cannot do. Once we get this truth into our being, our ministries will change and you will find a new freedom when it comes to healing. I have found incredible release in my limited years of ministering to people as a result of knowing that Jesus ministered as a human. It has given me great hope and confidence.

I know that much of what I'm saying in this book will seem simplistic; my point is to remind you of how simple healing is supposed to be. Every one of us is supposed to be able to heal! I have about 50 talks that all say the same thing: Jesus, even though he was fully God, did all his healings and miracles through the empowering of the Holy Spirit.

MIRACLES IN BRAZIL

At most meetings that I lead, we have a time to see if the principles I am writing about are true. I do this by asking those with sickness and pain to stand. At one large church in the south of Brazil God showed up big time.

The pastor there is a local hero. His church is the largest in his city. On top of that, he had started another 50 churches in his city and about 200 in his state. He also was an elected member of government. (I guess when everyone goes to your church it is easy to be voted into public office!)

This man is also anointed; he has built the kingdom in his region through powerful signs and wonders. People come to his meetings to meet God and receive healing. But he wasn't trained to release others to do the same. I asked his permission to have his church members do the ministry rather than follow the "anointed man/woman of God" model. He was skeptical, but agreed.

At the end of my sermon I felt the Lord saying to start with the harder cases, so I asked everyone to stand up who had any sort of eye problem. The meeting had about three thousand in attendance and my guess is over a hundred people stood up.

I had the person beside them place his/her anointed hands on the one standing and we prayed a simple prayer: "My healing belongs to me because of what Jesus has done, I receive my healing now!" Then I asked people to check their eyesight. Clapping began to breakout everywhere. Excitement rang through the room as people began to realize that something had happened. The tradition of this church was that their pastors sit on the stage with the senior pastor on a throne-style chair. The pastors were all intrigued as they watched their congregation minister healing.

I called everyone to the front who had been healed and more than 50 responded. I then asked the senior pastor, their local hero, to interview them. As one after another described serious eye problems, he kept turning to me to say, "he's healed!"

After the meeting, over a dinner of several small cows and pigs, the pastor was overwhelmed with how easy healing had been. He knew the ministry style that I did was different—they didn't do "body" ministry. He joked that I had trained his people to do better miracles than he could. He realized that the anointing was with his people, not just the leadership.

I CAN DO THAT!

I have the same opportunities to heal people as Jesus. When I read the Bible I used to think: *Wow, Jesus was good!* Now, when I read a story about the healing ministry of Jesus I say to myself: *I could do that.* Do you see the difference? Everything changed in terms of my confidence when I began to grasp that Jesus flowed in the same anointing of the Holy Spirit that you and I do.

Now when I read the Scriptures I look for the keys that Jesus used. As I write this, my spirit is bubbling up with excitement. I can feel the leap in my spirit knowing that I can do anything Jesus did. Not only that, but Jesus prophesied over me that I would do even greater miracles than he did (John 14:12). Yes, yes, yes! He says the same prophetic word over you as well!

The Bible is full of examples of the ordinary people God used to heal and do other great miracles. Philip is a great example of an ordinary person who God used to heal. Acts 8:7-8 tells us that *"many who were paralyzed or lame were healed. So there was great joy in that city."* Philip was a waiter by training, not a superstar apostle.

Peter and John's first healing was not a simple headache. The man had been crippled for 40 years. Imagine that you have just been empowered by the Holy Spirit (Acts 2). What test would let you know that your experience of being empowered by the Holy Spirit really took? How would you know if you were anointed? How about finding an extremely needy person, such as a cripple, and asking God to do a miracle? If God does it, you know that everything is possible. That is what these men did. They saw a man and thought, *Right then, let's test to see if the authority and power that Jesus gave us actually works.* With boldness they spoke to the man, grabbed his hand, and stood him up. The Bible says that as they were pulling him to his feet, he was instantly healed.

What I love about this story is that they had an *oops* moment. They spoke to the man to be healed as they had seen Jesus do. But nothing happened. Oops! That didn't deter Peter and John. They reached down and pulled the man up. When they engaged their faith a second time, by pulling him up, the miracle took place.

For some reason, there are many Christians who believe that Satan has all the power in ministry, and they have none. I have a big problem with this. Why would Jesus expect us to be able to do greater ministry than he did, if we can't access the same power and authority that he did? Why would God let Satan have spiritual weapons and still expect us to overcome and resist the enemy in our own strength?

God did not tease us by giving a mandate to minister in the power of the Holy Spirit, but then limiting that ministry to the generation that lived right after the death of Jesus. It continues to this day and we can partner with Holy Spirit to take advantage of it.

ORDINARY STUDENTS

One of my joys is to teach in our School of Ministry. Twice each year, young adults from around the world join Catch The Fire for five months. We train them to be like Jesus and to minister like Jesus. I teach the healing module over four days, three hours each day, and always incorporate practice time. We've had some spectacular healings right in the classroom.

One of the girls that we practiced with came forward to be healed of a severe allergy to horses. (It just so happened that the coming weekend was a mini-outreach where some of the students were going to minister at a ranch!) After her friend prayed for her, she asked how would she know if the prayer worked. Easy.

"When you get out of the car at the ranch," I told her, "take a deep breath. If you begin to sneeze, have a reaction of any kind, get back in the car. But if you have no problems, start to walk around the ranch, slowing moving towards the horses."

When she got there she had no reaction, even as she walked straight to the horses. This young lady eventually stood by a horse, touched it, and then went for her very first horse ride! God used her friends to heal her, just as we can be used to heal those in our lives.

The prayer of a righteous person is powerful and effective.
Elijah was a human being, even as we are. He prayed earnestly that it would not rain, and it did not rain on the land for three and a half years. Again he prayed, and the heavens gave rain, and the earth produced its crops. JAMES 5:16-18

The prayers of ordinary people work. In this passage, James is writing about healing the sick. Interestingly, he includes the story of Elijah. Elijah prayed that there would be no rain for three years. It didn't rain for three years until God told him to pray for rain to return—and it rained. The inclusion of Elijah in this passage serves to demonstrate the power of the prayers of ordinary people. Perhaps you are thinking that Elijah wasn't an ordinary man but an extraordinary one. You are partially correct. Elijah was an extraordinary man, but he also was crippled by depression, and in his later days he was disobedient to God. He had tremendous high points at the beginning of his ministry, but it would appear that he finished poorly.

While in depression, God asked him to complete three tasks, but sadly none of them were accomplished in the way God intended. You'll remember that he was asked to anoint two men as kings and to anoint Elisha as his successor (1 Kings 19:15-16). None of those things happened. Elisha had to contend for his anointing on Elijah's last day. While this may have had its benefits, the Lord had clearly asked Elijah earlier to simply anoint him, not make him jump through hoops for it.

Elijah's ups and downs show us just how ordinary he was. James, understanding that Elijah was just like us, says that ordinary is still okay. Ordinary is all it takes to be powerful and effective. I love this because it means that I qualify. That makes Elijah very much like you and me. We also have great potential and often get sidelined.

I believe that some reading this have given up hope that God hears their prayers. Some feel they have been disqualified. Some feel that it is too late to begin to believe. If God can use a depressed and disobedient servant like Elijah, he can use us!

God sees our prayers differently than we do. He considers our prayers powerful ones. God sees my feeble attempts to bring his kingdom to earth as effective. He sees my desire to do well and to see good things like healing happen to others. Most of us are alike in that we have had some periods of life where we are very close to God and others where we fail miserably. However, you and I don't have to have everything together in order to be used by God in a healing ministry.

James says that it is not just the elders who can minister healing, but rather we are to pray for each other. It would seem that God simply likes to honour our ordinary prayers. He sees them as good enough to activate healing. This shows us again that God is looking for anyone to agree with his desire to bring healing to a hurting person. Our Father is actively looking to partner with someone—anyone!

SAVED IN THE MORNING, HEALING IN THE AFTERNOON

My oldest son Jon is a worship leader, among other things. One of the bands at our church is a youth band called *The Freshwind Band.* Jon used to play with them. They did a bit of touring and one year played at a youth conference in Dallas, Texas. Jon told me that at one of the morning sessions a young girl from a punk rock lifestyle gave her life to Jesus. Very exciting!

In the afternoon, the youth who were attending the conference were sent out to do the Jesus stuff on the streets. This brand new believer was on a team. The girl, who had been saved for less than three hours, went out to minister healing and God answered her prayers! Did she say the right words? Probably not. But it didn't stop God's healing power—prayer works.

What qualifies us to minister healing?
Is it because healing has something to do with you and me? No.
Is it about how long we have known Jesus? No.
Is it about being male or female? No.
Is it about having a formal role in a church? No.

Healing is something everyone can do, and it's easy not because of us, but because of God. In the Christian realm, many feel that the prayers of pastors, priests, television personalities, or missionaries somehow get answered before those who are not "professionals." God knows that most of us are not clergy or elders. In fact, there is only one professional Christian for every 300 ordinary Christians. Very few of us make our living from being a follower of Jesus. God doesn't care; he loves to use the prayers of ordinary people.

LEGS LENGTHENED BY A FIVE-YEAR-OLD
Several years ago I was ministering in the middle of England near Barnsley.

Oliver and Jennifer Hall lead a church in the Partners in Harvest network of which Catch The Fire is also a member. I was there for just one night.

My recollection is that there were 30 people at the meeting. It was my first time there so no one knew me. Because it was a smaller group, I could be much more informal and instead of using words of knowledge I simply asked the people what their health issues were. One man told me that he had recently been in an accident. He was riding his motorcycle when the hood of an oncoming car flew up, blocking the view of other drivers. He was hit by a car and tossed on the road. The man had his leg broken from the crash with severe bone damage; his leg was reconstructed with bolts and pins. As they were putting the leg together they ran out of bone, so his injured leg was shorter than the undamaged one.

I asked if people had ever seen a leg grow. They hadn't. Neither had I, but I didn't say that. Faith came to me; this would not only be easy, but would be fun. So we sat him in a chair and I asked everyone to come forward and watch. I was just about to command the leg to straighten and grow when a thought jumped to my head: *How about if we have the pastor's five-year-old daughter do the prayer?*

I called her up and asked this sweet little girl if she would like to do the miracle. She said yes, and I told her what to do. She asked Jesus to straighten the man's leg and to make it longer. Then we all counted to three and yelled "Now!" Well, we had a mixture of crying and laughing for the next few minutes. The man's leg snapped into the right position and grew. He began to walk around, putting weight on it and jumping. He was healed!

I saw Pastor Oliver a few days later at one of our conferences and he told me that the man played football (soccer) with his son in their yard the very next day!

I want to encourage you to be bold and begin to pray for the sick. I believe that as you step out and minister you are sowing into your own future healing. People who believe in healing for others also end up believing in healing for themselves. As you learn to minister, you learn also how to receive ministry. Friends, we can all heal the sick because it is not us who is doing it. It is the Spirit of God in us! Let me pray for you.

Father, thank you that you have given your ministry of healing to us. Thank you that we get to represent you. Thank you that we can put our hands on the sick and they will be healed. Thank you that our prayers can bring life. Thank you that we can flow in your anointing even when we don't think we are. Father would you give boldness to each one? Would you give a greater anointing to each one? Inspire us to believe that we can minister just like Jesus did! Amen.

154

CHAPTER 6

How Jesus Ministered Healing

While Jesus was on earth, living as a man, he ministered healing to people exactly how God intends for us to minister. Jesus didn't come to earth just to die for our sins. If that had been the case, why delay the process for three years? Jesus also came to represent the Father on earth and show us how the Father wants us to act, talk, and minister healing. He spent three years teaching about the Kingdom and showing how the Kingdom had come to earth.

All that we need to know about how to minister healing can be seen in the life of Jesus. When we study it we begin to see nuggets of truth. We see the secrets to Jesus' success that often are overlooked. Not only did Jesus minister out of his humanity, but he expects us to do the same. This takes the pressure off us and puts it on God. Our part, as we have seen, is to simply obey the leadings of the Holy Spirit and step out in faith.

I have good news and bad news for you. First the bad news: there is no formula that Jesus used. There is no three-step pattern or a simple A-B-C model that we can copy time and time again. Now the good news: almost anything you do can be used to heal people! Bill Johnson says that Jesus is perfect theology. That means that anything Jesus said was right. Anything that Jesus did was right. We can never go wrong in copying Jesus.

A MOTIVATING FORCE

As we think about how Jesus ministered we need to first spend time on the topics of love, mercy, and grace. These were the reasons behind his actions as he ministered healing. Many of the healing accounts refer to compassion as his primary motivation.

> When Jesus heard what had happened, he withdrew by boat privately to a solitary place. Hearing of this, the crowds followed him on foot from the town. When Jesus landed and saw a large crowd, he had compassion on them and healed their sick. MATTHEW 14:13-14

The Greek word for *compassion* implies a state of turmoil within the inner being of Jesus. When he saw the crowds, who had interrupted his private retreat with the Twelve, his heart went out to them. Their needs began to overshadow his needs. He changed his agenda based on the stirring in his inner being.

Similarly in Luke 7, we read of Jesus coming into the town of Nain with a large crowd. As he is about to enter the village, another large crowd is leaving. This one is not as joyous and upbeat as the crowd with Jesus. It is the funeral procession of the only son of a widow. Her primary support was gone; life would be very tough for her from then on. Verse 13 says, "*When the Lord saw her, his heart went out to her and he said, 'Don't cry.'*" Do you feel what Jesus felt? Can you imagine the turmoil that was stirring in his heart?

Compassion compelled Jesus to action. He was driven by the stirrings of injustice that the Holy Spirit put in his heart. Friends, this is a key for us to catch. When your heart is filled with compassion that usually means that God is positioning you for a ministry opportunity.

Let's look at another story. In Matthew 20:34, Jesus met two blind men on the road to Jericho. You'll remember that they cried out for mercy but the crowds tried to hush them. "*Jesus had compassion on them and touched their eyes. Immediately they received their sight and followed him.*" Compassion motivated Jesus to action. They cried out for mercy, and Jesus, feeling something in the pit of his stomach, acted.

Here is one more story, from Mark 9:22. There was a son, a young boy, who was demonized and in desperate need of help. The father had gone to the disciples, who had stayed behind while Jesus was on a mountain being glorified with Moses and Elijah. The nine disciples who stayed behind had not been able to help and so the father came to Jesus upon his return. Notice the words the father spoke: "*If you can do anything, take pity on us and help us.*"

The father appealed to the compassion in Jesus. The word *pity* is the same Greek word as *compassion*, just translated differently in this passage. Perhaps he had heard the stories of Jesus helping others in great times of need. Perhaps he knew that if he pushed that mercy button, Jesus would stop and act. Sure enough, God moved Jesus' heart.

Friends, this is a simple lesson for us. Whenever you see a need and your heart goes out to the person, recognize that God is trying to get your attention. You have probably felt that tug many times when you've seen a handicapped person, a person suffering from AIDS, or a child with leukemia. Compassion is God's way of getting you to act. He is using it to cause you to react to injustice. Your spirit knows that this situation is just not right. God wants you to do something about it!

Even those who don't know Jesus respond to compassion. Every year, millions of dollars are given to telethons and appeals focusing on the diseases and physical needs of people. We hear their stories, we see their needs, and we give money. If God got the attention and subsequent action of Jesus this way, it is a sure bet that he will also use this technique with you and me. He is the healer, but he wants to partner with us to be the ones who touch or speak on his behalf. He is desperate to partner with someone to bring about healing.

Heidi Baker has to be the poster girl for God's compassion. I've had the opportunity to be with her in Mozambique several times. I've seen how she ministers; she usually comes to our church at least once a year, often twice. In Mozambique, she talks to every single person when she is on a walk. As the people recognize her she stops, hugs them, and talks to them.

She asks about their children, their parents, and their spouses. She prays for them and they love her for it. I've seen her at Catch The Fire Toronto spending hours with just one or two people. She finds the hurting and lonely and begins to love them to life. She lives for the one!

Let's give God permission to stir compassion in us when he wants us to represent him:

> *Father, we want to be like Jesus. We know you want us to represent you. Father, there were many times when the way you got the attention of Jesus was by stirring his emotions. Would you do the same for us? Would you so move us that we are compelled to act? Father, help us never to give in to the fears of others, to disappointments from the past, or to other excuses that keep us from getting up and doing something. Father, we are tired of knowing what you want and hesitating. Would you help us to never doubt, never question, and never miss the opportunities you have for us. We welcome you to cause turmoil in our innermost being. Help us recognize this as a signal from you. We pray this in the name of Jesus, amen.*

A HEALING TOUCH

The most common method that Jesus used in his healing ministry was to touch people. As he put his hands on people, the power of God went from him into the person to whom he was ministering. Jesus touched lepers, touched the lame, touched the multitudes, etc., but in Matthew 9 he was asked to touch a dead girl and bring her back to life.

While he [Jesus] was saying this, a ruler came and knelt before him and said, "My daughter has just died. But come and put your hand on her, and she will live." Jesus got up and went with him, and so did his disciples ... When Jesus entered the ruler's house and saw the flute players and the noisy crowd, he said, "Go away. The girl is not dead but asleep." But they laughed at him. After the crowd had been put outside, he went in and took the girl by the hand, and she got up. News of this spread through all that region. **18-19,23-26**

We've already looked at the story of Jairus and the healing of his daughter, but let's take a closer look at the specifics. When he comes to Jesus what Jairus asked for was a touch. It would appear that even though he may not have been a follower of Jesus, he knew the primary way in which Jesus ministered. In Matthew 8:3, Jesus touched a leper, without fear that he would contract leprosy. Rather, he was confident that the healing anointing in him would overpower the devastating effects of the disease.

It would also appear that because touching was the primary method Jesus used for healing people, that the early church leaders copied this. The first healing in Acts occurred when Peter and John grabbed the hand of a lame man (Acts 2:7). The next healing that is described is when Ananias ministered to Saul (Acts 9:17) for his blindness by placing his hands on Saul.

In the ministry of Jesus, touching is mentioned more than any other form of impartation. Putting your hands on someone also became the primary way for people to impart the empowering of the Holy Spirit (Acts 8:17). It is the way that we anoint people for leadership (Acts 6:6), and release gifts of the Spirit into someone (2 Timothy 1:6). There is something special that happens when a believer in Jesus touches another person. Touches impart life.

ANDREW'S STORY

I remember a Sunday at our church when Mary Audrey Raycroft, one of our Catch The Fire Toronto pastors, had a word of knowledge about a man being in a winter-related accident three days prior. One of the men in our congregation responded at the urging of his wife and limped to the front of the auditorium wearing a Velcro leg cast and a knee brace, hobbling on crutches.

Andrew had been in a skiing accident and torn the ACL in his left knee. I happened to be in the front row, along with others of our leadership team, and went over to minister healing while Mary Audrey continued preaching. The Holy Spirit visibly came on Andrew and I said, "You know that you're going to have to take that brace off to see if you've been healed, don't you?" He smiled and agreed to test his knee.

Within a few moments the brace and cast were off. We asked Andrew to test to see if he could bend his knee. He could, but still with stiffness. Several minutes later we had him standing, then walking tentatively. Finally, we told him to go for a slow walk around the sanctuary. Andrew heard the Lord tell him to run. He was hesitant, but gave it a go. He began to run! Mary Audrey had to pause her talk, which happened to be about the healing of a crippled lady (Luke 13). Our church stood to applaud a wonderful healing miracle that was taking place in front of our eyes.

My point in this story and that of Jairus' is this: touch is a very valid way to minister to people who are sick and needing healing. Jairus had probably seen this pattern in the ministry of Jesus and specifically requested a touch for his dead daughter. Do not be afraid to touch people as you minister healing. Touch literally connects you to that person and allows the anointing of God to pass from you into their body. It is a powerful tool to use when God calls you to pray for people who are sick.

A HEALING WORD

The second most frequent way in which we see Jesus ministering is through spoken words. We've already looked at the story of the centurion's servant who was healed in Matthew 8. Again, let's take a closer look at the specifics; there were several kinds of words given by Jesus, with commands and declarations being the two most common.

> *When Jesus had entered Capernaum, a centurion came to him, asking for help. "Lord," he said, "my servant lies at home paralyzed and in terrible suffering." Jesus said to him, "I will go and heal him." The centurion replied, "Lord, I do not deserve to have you come under my roof. But just say the word, and my servant will be healed."...Then Jesus said to the centurion, "Go! It will be done just as you believed it would." And his servant was healed at that very hour.*
> MATTHEW 8:5-8,13

Notice in this passage that what the centurion really wanted was for Jesus to *"say the word, and my servant will be healed."* He had such confidence in the words of Jesus that a trip to the house was not needed. A simple word would do! Jesus responds in like faith and simply says, *"Go! It will be done just as you believed it would."* The centurion takes him at his word and heads off. The Scriptures say, *"his servant was healed at that very hour."* This was a word of declaration.

Notice that Jesus does not say, "I will go and pray for his healing." Rather, he says, "*I will go and heal him.*" Never once do we see Jesus asking God to heal anyone. Rather, we see Jesus pronouncing a person healed. He commands demons to leave. His words are short and to the point. Most of his "prayers" are less than three words!

Having said this, we are definitely allowed to pray for people. As James points out (James 5:14–16), we are able to call out to God. My point is that this isn't how Jesus ministered. Praying, in one sense, shows that we aren't confident about what is going to happen. Jesus always knew what the outcome was going to be. He knew that each and every person he ministered to would be healed. My hope is that you and I will begin to move in our authority more frequently and speak things as though they are, rather than speaking as we'd like them to be.

Jesus also used verbal commands for sickness to leave. Matthew 8:16 tells us of a large healing meeting that Jesus had outside Peter's home in Capernaum, on the north shore of the Sea of Galilee. The Bible says, "*Many who were demon-possessed were brought to him, and he drove out the spirits with a word and healed all the sick.*" Jesus drove out the spirits that were causing the sickness with a word. We don't know what the word was, but if we look at what happened earlier that day in the synagogue we get a glimpse of what could have been said.

In Mark 1:25 we hear Jesus' word to a demonized man. "*'Be quiet!' said Jesus sternly. 'Come out of him!'*" As we look at the other gospel accounts of Jesus' ministry we see this was a common pattern. He spoke short statements, short commands, all with authority and power.

Jesus' words carried power; every person he spoke healing to received their healing. When he spoke to the lame man by the pool in John 5, he said, *"Get up! Pick up your mat and walk"* (John 5:8). The very next verse records the result, *"At once the man was cured"* (v. 9).

BARRIERS TO MINISTERING IN POWER AND AUTHORITY

This is the pattern every time, whether a command or a declaration. People were healed instantly when he spoke a healing word. This is the barrier that those of us who are called to a healing ministry come up against:

Do I have the authority to say the same kind of words?
Do I believe healing can be that easy?
Do I have the boldness to speak and step back and watch God work?

I would love to move in greater authority in this area. There have been times when I've clearly heard from God to speak a word of command and done just this. I was once asked to minister at an Elim Pentecostal church in Newcastle, England led by Simon Lawton. I'd met Simon earlier when he had been pastoring in the middle of England. He wanted to have me come and do a Holy Spirit meeting to help set the tone for his ministry at his new church.

After my talk I led a healing time. I asked people to stand if they had pain, and many did. I asked the people around them to find out what was wrong. Next I had them all speak my favourite healing prayer over the person in pain. They said, "Your healing belongs to you because of what Jesus has done. Receive your healing now!" A short command and declaration that healing is God's will. Folks were asked to check themselves and to come to the front and give a short testimony. The third person to share said that their shoulder was feeling much better. Only one problem, and it was a big problem: the man sharing was obviously blind. He was at the front with a guide dog. I hadn't seen the man nor the dog in the meeting. Because he didn't have pain in his eyes, he hadn't mentioned that to the woman who was ministering to him.

Well, I thought it would be a good thing to have a go at his eyesight. I asked who had commanded the pain to go in his shoulder; it was a gal in her twenties. It turns out that she wasn't a member of the church, but a guest. Also she wasn't yet a follower of Jesus. It didn't seem to bother God that a young woman who wasn't born again could successfully say a healing word over someone, so I invited her to help me minister to the blind man. We spoke to his eyes and commanded them to open; he said that he could see light.

We spoke God's will again; he could see shapes and forms.
We spoke again and he said he could see people, but blurry.
We prayed again and this time he said he could see clearly! Wow. Everyone was excited for the man. He was a part of their church and they all knew him. It was wonderful!

I can be a bit of a joker in meetings. I think Jesus liked to have fun while he was ministering, so I try to not be too serious. We got a book that was in the front row and gave it to him to see if he was telling the truth. He took off his dark sunglasses and proceeded to read a paragraph. There were lots of tears that night. God responded to our commands. May we be bold enough to minister with the same authority as Jesus.

HEALING REVELATION

Knowledge gives us an advantage. Information is absolutely vital in today's world. Companies strive to be one step ahead of their competitors. Information and knowledge often separate the winners from the losers.

Jesus, it would appear, had inside information that enabled him to minister in strength, boldness, and confidence. He always seemed to know what God was up to. The Scriptures say that, *"Jesus knew that the Father had put all things under his power, and that he had come from God and was returning to God"* (John 13:3). When he was about to be arrested, John records that *"Jesus, knowing all that was going to happen to him, went out and asked them, 'Who is it you want?'"* (John 18:4). And on the cross itself, Scriptures say, *"knowing that everything had now been finished, and so that the Scripture would be fulfilled, Jesus said, 'I am thirsty'"* (John 19:28).

Knowledge comes to us in many forms. God gives us dreams. He speaks to us in visions. He gives us words of knowledge, words of wisdom, impressions, insights, understandings, etc. Jesus' ministry demonstrates that knowledge empowers us to be able to accomplish exactly what God wants. Because Jesus knew his Father's will, he always did what God wanted him to. He always said what God spoke to him, and always went where the Father wanted him to go. He acted according to the information he received from His Father. I'd like us to try to figure out how he got these revelations. If we can get that key, then we have the same opportunities to see miracles and healings.

I believe there were two primary ways that Jesus picked up the revelations which enabled him to represent Father. The first of these was through prayer. In Matthew 6, Jesus teaches his disciples about prayer. Note verse 8: "*Do not be like them, for your Father knows what you need before you ask him.*" I think Jesus is giving a very clear indication that prayer is one of the ways to determine what God wants. Prayer, as you know, is not a one-way street. It is a dialogue. I once played a trick in one of our leadership training classes at Catch The Fire. I was helping people to learn how to hear the voice of God specifically through writing in a journal. I had everyone get out a piece of paper and I asked each person to write a prayer of gratitude for two minutes.

After the two minutes I asked them to write this question: Father, what would you like to say to me? Everyone had an easy time writing the prayer and many surprised themselves as thoughts came to them in response to the question. I asked how many of them knew in advance what they would write on the paper. No one knew ahead of time; as they wrote, more ideas came.

Here is the trick: whether writing a prayer, or thoughts from God, they were tapping into revelation. They realized that even though they were talking to God, he was the one giving them the ideas of what to write. I believe this is what Jesus did every day. Whether it was the early mornings with the Father (Mark 1:35), or late at night (Mark 6:46), Jesus received insights from God as they communed.

WRONG QUESTION

We once had a young healing evangelist based in Canada. He was speaking at a gathering of Toronto pastors and a question was asked regarding revelation. A pastor asked, "How come I get information about people in the meetings, even the sickness they have, but, they are not healed?".

The evangelist replied, "You are asking the wrong question. Don't ask who is sick in the meeting, ask God whom he wants to heal in the meeting." Bingo! God has the answers if we ask the right questions.

Please do not think that Jesus was omniscient like our heavenly Father is. In his divinity he was, but remember that Jesus emptied himself of the use of this attribute. If Jesus had been all knowing, why then did he pray? Why did he not know that the lady who was hemorrhaging was about to touch him? He needed his Father to give him revelation. Without it, he had no idea this lady was sneaking up on him. Jesus was absolutely dependent on Holy Spirit for everything. He modeled *how to* in all areas, including how to get revelation.

WE HEAR BY TUNING IN

The second way that Jesus picked up revelation was by always being tuned to the Spirit. Jesus lived in the spirit realm. He would see in the Spirit.

He would hear in the Spirit. It would appear that Jesus spent time asking his Father for revelation. What he didn't get in his prayer times, the Father filled in as the day went on. That is exactly how it is supposed to work for you and me. God loves to communicate so that his will can be accomplished on earth just like it is in heaven. He has a vested interest in seeing his plans done his way. He could just go about zapping things into being, but that is not his style. He almost always works through people like you and me.

Want more revelation? Want more insights into the day ahead of you? Do the same two things as Jesus did. Plan to meet with the Revealer and plan to tune in to his wavelengths throughout your whole day.

I was ministering in Scotland recently at a Partners in Harvest mini-conference. I was leading a healing time after my talk. As I was finished I asked for those with potentially life-threatening diseases to come forward. Two ladies stood and it just happened that both had multiple sclerosis. Before I began to minister, each of them told the gathering what their negative symptoms were. They said things like imbalance, headaches, pain, etc. I prayed for them and asked the anointing to kick in. No change. I cancelled demonic spirits. Still no change. As I was about to give up a thought came to me: *Bless their spirits.* I explained to them that although God speaks to our spirit, we can have a wounded spirit or a crushed spirit that can block the revelation. Karen, the older of the two women, didn't understand what I was saying so I repeated myself and added what I thought was a made-up example. What actually happened was that an example spontaneously came to my mind and I simply said it.

I told Karen that if she had loved painting as a child and wanted to pursue that as a career, but her parents had suppressed her enthusiasm, it was possible her spirit had been crushed. Well, that example hit the spot! Karen cried out in deep emotional pain and crumpled to the ground. Turns out my made-up example wasn't made up at all—it was instant revelation from my Father. Karen had wanted to be a painter and her parents had forced her to give up her dreams. Wow!

Karen was at the meeting I was leading the next night and she shared that she had been symptom-free for 24 hours. The knowledge that God gave me spoke specifically to Karen and released life and healing to her. It was the specific way the Father wanted Karen healed. I don't know why a touch didn't heal her. I don't know why a command hadn't helped. What I do know is that the Father spoke to me when I was searching for an answer to help bring healing to her. God gave me the thought to pray for her spirit. He then followed that by giving me the example of her being a painter. I simply shared the revelation that came to me.

THE GIFTS OF THE SPIRIT

I've already made pointed out that Jesus didn't use his own divine abilities when it came to ministry. He set an example of how to do healing with Holy Spirit as the source of power and authority. He chose to partner with Holy Spirit, just we are supposed to. He excelled in every aspect of each gifting and showed us how to use the various gifts in a healing ministry.

On a Sabbath Jesus was teaching in one of the synagogues, and a woman was

*there who had been crippled by a spirit for eighteen years. She was bent over
and could not straighten up at all. When Jesus saw her, he called her forward
and said to her, "Woman, you are set free from your infirmity." Then he put
his hands on her, and immediately she straightened up and praised God.* LUKE
13:10–13

Luke is the only author to record this healing. It reveals how Jesus flowed
in his use of the gifts of the Spirit. One of my favourite preachers at Catch
The Fire is Mary Audrey Raycroft. She is a wonderful expositor of the
Scriptures and preached a sermon on this passage. In the talk, she spoke
on how Jesus used five of the gifts of the Spirit as he healed this lady. The
first gift Jesus used was word of knowledge. The passage says that Jesus
"saw her." He knew about this lady and what was wrong, even before he
met her, thanks to the Holy Spirit. Words of knowledge like this generally
come to people in one of three ways: hearing, seeing, or sensing. Jesus
functioned in the same way. John's gospel records that Jesus said he could
only do what he *heard*, what he *saw*, and what he was *taught*.

Next, Jesus used the gift of wisdom; he decided what to do with the information. He *"called her forward"* and *"put his hands on her."* Jesus did this on
the Sabbath in full view of his critics.

The third gift he flowed in was faith. In calling her forward, Jesus imparted
faith to this lady and she responded in faith. Because she believed Jesus,
she was able to do what he said to do. Jesus flowed in the gift of discernment to identify the specific cause of the lady's problem: a spirit of infirmity
that had crippled her for eighteen years. Her problem was not an accident
or a birth defect, it was a demonic spirit that was assigned to cripple her.

Jesus then used two gifts in partnership with each other: the gift of healing and the gift of miracles. I'm not sure if this was a great healing or a
low-level miracle, but the demonic spirit left instantly when Jesus spoke
the word of release. Luke says, "*He put his hands on her, and immediately
she straightened up and praised God.*" Healing anointing passed through the
words and touch of Jesus into the lady and she was restored. The crowds
were amazed and the religious leaders were upset. Another normal day
for Jesus!

Friends, we are designed to function in the very same way as Jesus did.
We are designed to sense the leading of the Holy Spirit and to use the
supernatural gifts of God. Understand that we are partners with Holy
Spirit. He does all the hard parts and allows us to do the fun part; namely
the speaking or touching. We get to be the visible doers of what Holy
Spirit invisibly does. We are the ones who get the quiet nudges and the
impressions of what to do and say.

I don't think that Jesus knew when he was switching from one gift to the
other. He simply flowed in unity with what his Father wanted. That will be
the way it is for us. I believe that the gifts are given to us when we need
them. Some of us seem to use one or two more often than others, yet when
we need them, they are all available to us.

Maybe this has happened to you: I'm ministering to someone who has pain
somewhere in his or her body and the pain moves. Their shoulder is pain
free, but now their back hurts. Over the years I've picked up knowledge
that this is a manifestation of a demonic spirit. The fact that the spirit has

moved tells me that it knows it is about to go, so I simply need to step into my authority and command it to go. This is how miracles and healings function. We use the various gifts to see people healed.

JAMES MALONEY

We've had James Maloney with us several times. One night in particular, he had a couple words of knowledge before he started to preach. He was right on both of them. He looked at a woman who was in the fourth row and said she had pain in her shoulder and it had been there for years. Was it now gone? Yes. He asked who in the crowd of five hundred had surgery on their leg from a football injury. A Nigerian man from our congregation came forward. He said that he had been a professional football (soccer) player and an injury had ended his career. Not only did James get the diagnosis right but also he even used the right word *football*, which to this man meant soccer.

After teaching for a while James began to read what he was seeing in the spirit. It was like there was a projection screen. He called up people who matched what he saw and accurately read their mail. After twenty minutes of that he moved into the gift of faith. He sat on a stool and laid hands on the rest of the people who wanted healing. I stood beside him as I do for most guest speakers. (I'm looking to learn how they minister.)

I remember Keith and Eleanor Sproule, a couple from our Brampton campus, being in line. Eleanor was dying from Lou Gehrig's disease and in her last days. She sat in a wheelchair breathing with the help of an oxygen machine. She didn't look good.

James asked her a pointed question: Did she want to be healed or was she ready to go and be with Jesus? She said she wasn't ready to die but wanted to live another year. So he agreed with her, laid his hands on her, and said a prayer. Within one week Eleanor greatly improved. She lived for one more year; dying almost to the day of the prayer. I talked to Keith, her husband recently. We both commented that when Eleanor had said she wanted another year that neither of us had picked up on that. We both would have been happy for another week. We should have interrupted her and said ten more years!

HEALING FROM A DISTANCE

There are very two interesting stories relating to Jesus ministering to sick people who were not with him at the time. The one mentioned below and the story of the centurion who had a suffering servant at his home. In both instances the son and servant were healed at the very moment Jesus spoke the healing word.

And there was a certain royal official whose son lay sick at Capernaum. When this man heard that Jesus had arrived in Galilee from Judea, he went to him and begged him to come and heal his son, who was close to death. "Unless you people see signs and wonders," Jesus told him, "you will never believe." The royal official said, "Sir, come down before my child dies."

"Go," Jesus replied, "your son will live." The man took Jesus at his word and departed. While he was still on the way, his servants met him with the news that his boy was living. When he inquired as to the time when his son got better,

they said to him, "Yesterday, at one in the afternoon, the fever left him." Then
the father realized that this was the exact time at which Jesus had said to him,
"Your son will live." So he and his whole household believed. JOHN 4:46-54

There are two things that I'd like to draw to your attention to: first, healing from a distance is not only possible, it's no different than healing in person. Second, Jesus understood that there were different levels of healings. Jesus did not fret about the prospect of his first long distance healing. He knew that he was not the one who was doing it; therefore, he didn't need to be there in person. It demonstrated an amazing level of confidence in God's ability and willingness to heal. Jesus knew that a word commanded from a distance could heal just as easy as a personal touch. His statement to the royal official, perhaps the mayor, was that of absolute confidence in God's ability to minister to his son. Knowing that the Father's desire allowed Jesus to speak a simple word command: *"Go, your son will live."*

Confidence is an area of potential growth for those of us in ministry. We need to know that that God always wants people healed. Once we get confident of that, things such as distance and level of sickness are no longer obstacles. Jesus never got worried about the severity of a person's illness.

This son was nearing death; it didn't matter.
This son was in a distant city; it didn't matter.

Do you begin to see how Jesus ministered? He had absolute confidence in both the desire of his Father to heal and his ability to be the agent of healing! With those two items stored inside the mind and heart of Jesus, it was game on.

Let's talk about the levels of healings. In this passage Jesus is clearly linking what is about to happen as a miraculous sign. Signs are designed to point people in a certain direction. Jesus is acknowledging that some healings serve that purpose. Healing someone from a distance has a greater impact than healing a person standing in front of you. By its very nature, this kind of healing drew more attention to the Jesus, who healed in a way no one had seen before.

Why did Jesus do this healing? Signs and wonders are purposefully designed to shake our mindsets. This miracle was done as much for the sake of the official (and his families and servants), as it was for the dying son. It was to help them believe in who Jesus was. When we minister, part of the purpose of healing is to show people that Jesus is alive. It also communicates to people that God loves them; he is powerful and able to intervene in their lives. If we take the credit for healing them, we will look good in the eyes of people, but, if we make Jesus look good, people will give their lives to him!

HEALING OVER THE PHONE

Several years ago we had a great healing conference featuring people like Bill Johnson and Todd Bentley. Todd had asked the people to call friends on the phone who needed a miracle. People were being healed over the phone. At one point one of the girls in our School of Ministry came to me. She asked if I would be willing to pray for her brother who was at home. The mom didn't want to wake up the brother so we agreed to pray with her on his behalf.

Did I tell you yet that he was autistic and had never talked? Does that change things? I had never seen an autistic person healed, nor even heard of such a healing before. Does that change things? Not at all! The mother, sister, and I all agreed that a miracle could take place. I don't remember my prayer; it wasn't important what I said. The next day I saw the girl. She was all excited, jumping up and down, waiting to give me an update. It turns out that the boy who was asleep while we were praying, who didn't hear the prayer, who wasn't at the anointed meeting, and who doesn't even know who I am, came downstairs on the Saturday morning talking. His sister said that he had been completely healed!

Don't ever let distance limit you. If God is putting an opportunity in front of you, respond in faith regardless of the obstacles and you will see great miracles.

MEETING A NEED

Matthew's gospel lumps many Jesus' healing stories together and, in some cases, out of sequence. His point isn't when, but why. One of the key points that I believe Matthew was seeking to make was that Jesus ministered according to need. Ministering healing was so much a part of the day-to-day life of Jesus that he never gave it a second thought. He never stopped to pray and ask his Father if he should minister healing; he just knew to do it.

Consider the Matthew 8 account of Jesus healing a man with leprosy, the suffering servant, and Peter's mother-in-law. The principle is the same in each of these three stories. They came and asked for help because they had a need, and Jesus ministered to those needs every time. Jesus didn't have prior knowledge of what the day was going to bring. He simply responded to needs and in each case that meant healing. You and I will find ourselves in similar situations. We'll be at work, in a crowded mall, at a church meeting, or taking the dog for a walk. We'll see someone with a need. Unless you have the same reputation that Jesus did, you probably won't be asked to step in and minister. We will need to be the ones to initiate the process.

I've found that the best way to minister is to just jump in headfirst. I usually begin the conversation by saying something like this: "I couldn't help but notice that your son is wearing a cast and seems to be in pain. I'm a follower of Jesus and while I was walking by I felt God ask me to come over and heal your son. Would you mind if I pray for him?"

I've rarely had people say no. I think most are a bit shocked and overwhelmed, especially when the healing takes place. I can't think of any times where I have prayed for a person I approached and nothing positive happened. In every case something good happens. The pain leaves or is leaving. Often the person is instantly healed.

I remember being in a shopping mall once and seeing a lady with a limp. I went over to her and asked what had happened. She told me that she'd had an accident and her leg was in severe pain. I asked if I could say a prayer for her and she was okay with that. She repeated my little prayer: "My healing belongs to me, because of what Jesus has done, I receive my healing now." She was healed instantly! She then asked me how much I charged for healing her. I told her it was free, that I did it as a follower of Jesus because he cares for hurting people. She told me that she had been paying good money to have physiotherapy and wanted to give me some money. Again I told her no. She proceeded to get out her checkbook and ask for my name. I said I wasn't going to do that. She then wrote something on the check, folded it and put it in my pocket and walked away with no limp.

What would you do? Well I turned the other way, went around a corner and got the check out.

A thousand dollars! It cashed!

Too often my problem is that I don't do anything. I let fears and doubts stop me. I listen to the lies of Satan:

> *You misheard God. He just wants you to intercede privately.*
> *What will they think when nothing happens?*
> *They don't want to talk to strangers.*

It's these very thoughts that usually confirm I initially heard God right—he is asking me to step out and Satan is trying to talk me out of it. There are two things I'd like to pray for as we get near the end of this book. First, for you to see the needs of others. Second, to have the boldness and desire to step in and minister to the needy.

> *Father, we believe that your Son was our model for healing ministry.*
> *It would appear from the gospel stories that he always responded in*
> *the affirmative when faced with a need. Father, would you help us to*
> *have the same heart to help your people? Would you cause our eyes,*
> *ears, and heart to be sensitive to what is happening in the lives of those*

around us? Father, give us supernatural boldness when it comes to introducing ourselves and to ministering in public places. Father, you gave boldness to Peter, John, and the others gathered in Acts 4. Would you please give us more boldness so that we can represent you just like Jesus did? In the name of Jesus we pray, amen.

CHAPTER 7

Tapping Into Restorative Powers

There is an interesting omission in all the stories about healing. There is no record of these people teaching others how they ministered healing. Whether it's Jesus, Peter, Paul, or any of the Old Testament giants like Moses, Elijah, Elisha—they left us no healing 101 notes to help us. Just as we did in the previous chapter, it's up to us to look for keys in the Scriptures to discover how these people ministered.

James, the pastor and apostolic leader of the church in Jerusalem, is the exception. In a few succinct verses found in James 5, the author gives us much to chew on in terms of how to heal and receive healing. His secret is tapping into restorative powers that are already waiting for us.

Is anyone of you sick? He should call for the elders of the church to pray over him and anoint him with oil in the name of the Lord. And the prayer offered in faith will make the sick person well; the Lord will raise him up. If he has sinned, he will be forgiven. Therefore confess your sins to each other and pray for each other so that you may be healed. The prayer of a righteous man is powerful and effective. JAMES 5:14–16

Before we get into the meat of this passage, let's back up and talk about James. Jacob was his real name. When the Bible was being translated for the common English folk, the king, James, who was sponsoring the project asked that his name be included in the Bible, so a couple of Jacobs were changed to James. Jacob the disciple became James, and Jacob the half-brother of Jesus became James. This James didn't always believe that Jesus was the Anointed One. He and the rest of his family were not so sure at times who Jesus was. Once, they came to take him away, probably to talk some "sense" into him (John 7:5).

We don't know when, but at some point James went from being agnostic to believing that Jesus was Lord. My guess is that this happened when the apostles began to take the Kingdom message on the road. James' authority grew and he became the leader of the church in Jerusalem; when a key decision needed to be discussed, James was the presiding bishop (Acts 15). He gave the final say on the matter and made sure that the decision was dispatched to the Christian churches.

There are some that teach that James' book is not written to believers and that we who are followers of Jesus don't have to abide by his wisdom. I disagree completely. God gives *all* scripture for the benefit of all believers (2 Timothy 3:16). Those who dislike James often take issue with his teaching that grace also includes doing things and working out our own salvation. Many miss the difference between the power of the sin and the penalty of sin. I personally believe that our penalty was fully paid for on the cross. However, getting out from under the power of sin is an ongoing process that requires us to rely on the Holy Spirit daily.

THE POWER OF ANOINTING

James is very simplistic and pragmatic. *"Are you sick? Call for the elders and they will pray for your healing"* (v. 14). James assumes that sick people will be made well when elders pray. He uses bold and positive phrases like *"will make the sick person well; the Lord will raise him up"* (v. 15). He is full of confidence in God's desire and ability to heal. For James, it is easy to believe that elders can do this simple task.

So who are these elders? Many churches don't use the term today, so let me give you some history. The word *elder* has two connotations in Scripture: the first has to do with age and wisdom, and the second has to do with roles and positions. Elders were often senior men who, because of their age, experience, and wisdom, had leadership roles. Over time, age wasn't always a factor; younger men or women were seen to possess the same characteristics and were added to leadership teams.

Paul told Timothy, a young man and leader of the world's largest church at the time, to not be quick to lay hands on someone (1 Timothy 5:22), in reference to giving away titles and responsibilities. People need to be proved able to function in key leadership roles.

Today, many use the word pastor, priest, vicar, minister, or leader to refer to the spiritual overseers of our congregations. Whatever word we use, James is saying that if you are sick, head to those with the most spiritual authority in your life. They are supposed to carry an anointing for ministering healing. This was not meant to be a superficial exercise or a tradition; praying for the sick isn't what you do so that the they feel the warm fuzzies. James tells us to have elders minister healing because the anointing works.

In our congregation in Toronto we have several levels of leadership. We have about 25 people who have the title of pastor. Some are full time and others part time. They function as elders in the biblical sense. We also have several hundred connect leaders. These men and women are all released to function as elders within the small groups/cells that they lead. We expect that all of our connect leaders can heal the sick through the anointing of the Holy Spirit and because of the atonement of Christ. We bless them to carry a healing anointing just like Jesus did. We also have a very large prayer ministry team. These are the men and women who minister at our Sunday meetings, special events, conferences, etc. As folks stand on the prayer lines the prayer team, functioning as elders, pray for and minister to the needs of the people.

James expected that the spiritual representatives of a church be able to heal because they carry an anointing. He assumed that your spiritual leader would be able to heal, because according to James, anointed, Spirit-filled people can help others with spiritual problems. James is saying, trust your leaders to know a bit more about healing than others do. It doesn't mean that they are better people, but their role as a spiritual leaders means that they should know how to address issues when they arise in the course of prayer ministry. James is not implying any "maybes" in this passage either; he has the utmost confidence that everyone, everywhere will be healed by their elders or their representatives because of the anointing they carry. They are to pray in faith and not doubt.

Often there is more to the prayer than just being healed; of the healings that Jesus participated in, almost one-third of them involved deliverance. A demonic spirit (or spirits) was often the root issue and when that was dealt with, the sickness or pain left. A couple of times Jesus dealt with sin issues first.

If you are in pain, or have sickness or disease in your body, I encourage you to do what the Bible says and ask your elder to lay hands on you for your healing and breakthrough. Every week, people come to our meetings at Catch The Fire, knowing that one of the "elders" will be leading the meeting and praying for the sick. Last Sunday it was my pleasure to lead a healing meeting; every person I ministered to was healed. Why? It is not because I'm a great man of God. It isn't because my prayers are better than others—people were also healed through the prayers of our ministry team. The reason everyone was healed is because they came in faith, knowing that healing prayers would be offered.

THE ROLE OF HONOUR

It is very interesting how ministers have more honour at another church, or in another country, than they do at home and their own church. Jesus experienced this. One of the reasons we bring in guest speakers is because people have a greater expectancy for other "elders." I recently had this happen to me. The host pastor had told people that I carry a healing anointing, so people needing healing came to the meeting.

One young man was about 35 and from Angola. He had been in a car accident in his home country. Doctors reconstructed his leg but made it slightly longer. He now had extreme arthritis in his rebuilt knee. The room was full of expectation; I had ministered in this African church once before, and people had been healed. On top of this, the man expected his healing, I expected his healing, and the pastor expected lots of healings.

His healing was recorded on video. His leg grew out and all the pain in his knee left. He has able to squat and jump around with absolutely no pain! He cried, I cried; we were all very happy that he had asked someone to minister. I was happy that God used me to be an elder and to minister to him in confidence. Sometimes bringing in an outsider opens doors to healing.

As an "elder" may I pray for your healing?

Father, James writes in these two short verses that people are to be healed through the prayers of elders. It is my privilege as an elder at Catch The Fire to pray for my friend today. I speak healing to you in the name of Jesus and command all pain to disappear now. I speak a release from every disease and sickness. I say that God intends for you to be healed today and I agree with the will of God for you. I bless your healing now in the mighty name of Jesus, amen!

THE POWER OF ANOINTING OIL

James tells us that when you are sick you should see an elder, preferably *your* elder. He also explains how this elder is to minister. There are two things that James says the elder is to do: use oil and pray in faith. We've talked a lot about faith already. Faith comes on the heels of revelation. When you get an *aha!* moment, hope follows. Hope encourages you but it doesn't heal you. Hope can heal you only if you do something with it—faith is the doing part.

A prayer of faith works the same way. The person praying has had a revelation about the person, the problem, or God and his will. Based on their revelation they are able to command for God's will to be done on earth, just like it would be in heaven. An example of a prayer of faith is *"My child, get up!"* (Luke 8:54). A normal prayer might be something like: "God would you please come and take away the sickness?" Do you see the difference? One prayer knows the outcome and the other prayer is simply is hoping for a healing.

The fact that anointing oil and praying in faith are combined gives us a hint as to what oil in this passage symbolizes. I've heard a lot of talks on this passage referring to oil as a medicinal agent for healing. In Mark 6:13 we read of how the Twelve *"drove out many demons and anointed many sick people with oil and healed them."* Oil does contain many properties that can aid in the healing process, but I think James is talking about something different. If oil by itself heals and is to be used by all believers, we should see more evidence of this. There is no record of Jesus ever using oil as a healing agent. If oil healing was the important clue in this passage, why doesn't James tell us what kind of oil to use? Do we use olive oil or olive oil with a myrrh and rose combination?

I personally believe that James is referring to oil as a symbol of the presence of the Holy Spirit. I am aware that when the Samaritan saw the Jewish man who had been mugged, he used oil and wine to help revive him (Luke 10:34). The guy who was mugged had oil smoothed into his body to help with pain and reduce infection. James doesn't refer to wine in this passage, so we are probably talking about something different.

Because James linked oil to prayer, we are better off understanding oil as symbolic of the Holy Spirit. When kings were crowned in the Old Testament, oil was used to symbolize the presence of God. When prophets and priests were initiated into ministry, oil was used as a sign of God's presence in their lives and future ministry. Without the Holy Spirit in your ministry you can put on a good show, but healings will not take place. The key to every healing is that God has to be present through the person of Holy Spirit.

As I mentioned before, there is no record of Jesus using oil to heal, nor do we have stories of Peter or Paul using oil. That doesn't mean that they didn't use oil from time to time. I think the emphasis that James is making is this: oil is an object lesson to remind us that the Holy Spirit's anointing has to be present for the sick to be healed. James was inviting God to be present. Combined with a prayer of faith, he says that people would be healed. The whole point of the passage is that people are supposed to get healed. I'm not sure if the oil was for the benefit of the person receiving prayer or for the person saying the prayer. Either way, both understood the point that they were tangibly inviting the presence of God.

SOME PRAYERS NEED AN EXTRA UMPH!

I'm reminded of the story of Jesus after he came down from the Mount of Transfiguration. Jesus met a father who asked him to heal his epileptic son. The man had already gone to his other nine disciples and that they had been unable to help the boy (Matthew 17:16). After healing the boy, Jesus rebuked his men for their lack of faith. When they later asked why they couldn't heal this boy, Jesus said they needed more intensity. These kinds of spirits only leave when you are prayed up; they needed to pray more and fast more.

Had the disciples assumed that since Jesus could heal everyone they also could, just by touching people? Was Jesus saying that simply by doing a six-day fast you could heal epileptics? I think his disciples had begun to minister to the boy without understanding that Jesus carried the presence of God. Their words apparently had no authority, and combined with the fact that Jesus wasn't there, they were powerless.

Friends, the prayers for healing by your elders need two things to work: the words they say need to be said in faith with a conviction that it is God's will for this person to be healed. Not later, but immediately! That is the prayer of faith. Second, their words need to be combined with an invitation for the Holy Spirit to come. Always remember to welcome the Holy Spirit when you minister to others, whether you say the words out loud or simply think them. He represents our Father on earth today. As God's agent of healing, the Holy Spirit comes where and when he is welcomed.

One of my worst ministry moments took place at a friend's church. I entered the meeting ready to go; I had a carload of eager School of Ministry students with me and they were prayed up. I remember praying and seeking God. As we prepared for ministry we all were drawn to a man who had crutches. I called him up to do a bit of show and tell. My intent was to show the church, who were not sympathetic to having a healing meeting, how easy it was.

Well the guy never got healed. In fact, he asked if he could return to his seat. Things got worse when a different man asked if he could be prayed for, but wasn't healed either. God did turn it around in the end once I switched to having people pray for each other. God was gracious and touched people at that point, but no one was healed by my words or my touches. At the end of the meeting, I had a one-on-one with God: *Where were you?* I felt God speaking a mild rebuke back to me: *It sounded to me like you knew what you were doing so I decided to watch you.* Ouch!

Never get too big for God. Stay small in his eyes and in your own. Make sure to always rely on the anointing to come and do what God intended for the anointing to do.

THE POWER OF FORGIVENESS

This probably should have been the very first chapter. I say this because forgiveness is one of the most powerful healing weapons we have! There is incredible power in forgiving others, yourself, and God.

Unforgiveness, in my humble opinion, is the main reason why Christians have pain and sickness in their lives. Unforgiveness is a plague on our nations. It plays right into the hands of Satan, who is desperate for us to empower him and give him a reason to bring sickness and suffering into our lives. When we don't forgive he is given that right.

James says that the elders are to ask one simple question when seeking to determine if there are any blockages to healing: Who do you need to forgive? If someone has sinned by not forgiving, then the elders are to lead him/her through the forgiveness process. Every one of us has prayed the Lord's Prayer over and over again:

> Forgive us our debts, as we also have forgiven our debtors ... For if you forgive
> men when they sin against you, your heavenly Father will also forgive you.
> But if you do not forgive men their sins, your Father will not forgive your sins.
> MATTHEW 6:12,14-15

Forgiveness is two-sided. When we forgive, we are forgiven. When we don't forgive, we aren't forgiven. There is something very dangerous that happens when we don't forgive another person. First, we quench the Holy Spirit and he backs off. Second, Satan jumps in and takes that ground, making the matter much worse.

I have a project for someone with time on his or her hands. My guess is that every war started with a small issue that someone didn't forgive. Because Satan got in the mix, the small offence became a big issue. The big issue became a diplomatic challenge. Pride got involved and before anyone knew it, a battle was on. Apologizing is a powerful weapon.

When people forgive they are often instantly healed. So much so that I

know what to do anytime I pray for a person and they aren't healed immediately. I push the forgiveness button and ask, "Is there someone you need
to forgive?"

Perhaps the most dynamic example of this was when I was with John
and Carol Arnott in Frederick, Maryland. We were there for several days
of meetings, and on the first evening John asked for those who had been
involved in accidents at least twenty years ago to come forward. One of the
men who responded was in his late seventies or eighties. John interviewed
him and we found out that 50 years ago he had been walking in a ditch
beside a road while a co-worker was driving a tractor. Through negligence,
the driver lost control and the tractor tipped over and landed on him. For
50 years this man had severe back pain.

The obvious question was had he forgiven the driver of the tractor? When
John asked the question, the man said, "No, and I'm not about to!" I think
everyone was a bit taken back by his statement. John asked him why, and
the man talked about all the misery he had experienced throughout his
life; he held this tractor driver responsible for it. John then asked another
simple question:

"Don't you think it is about time to give the man a gift he doesn't deserve
before he dies?" He thought about that for a few seconds and agreed that
he would release him. John led him through a simple prayer to forgive the
negligent tractor driver. There was no prayer for back pain, simply a prayer
to forgive his former co-worker. At the end of the prayer John told the man
to try to touch his toes.

His response was classic: "You didn't pray for my back to be healed."

John said, "I don't need to, your prayer to forgive did that." He began to bend over and to everyone's amazement he was able to bend all the way over. He touched his toes and came up smiling—no pain in his back at all!

The funniest part of this story was his daughter. She was in her fifties and was standing beside her dad the whole time. She fainted on the spot seeing her dad do something she had never witnessed in her life. Everyone had both tears of joy, because of the healing, and tears of laughter, as a result of seeing the daughter faint. Only God!

I've seen John Arnott minister like this for years. He'd call out all those injured in an accident twenty years ago or more and sure enough most would have a breakthrough after forgiving. I used to think how courageous John was that he would risk praying for these "hard" cases. Then one day as I was pondering forgiveness I got a revelation. John Arnott wasn't some super risky, push-the-envelope revival leader. He was simply assuming that if someone still had pain after twenty years they probably had unforgiveness. When I figured this out I said something like, "Why didn't you tell me how easy this type of healing is?" He just smiled at me. The rascal!

Friends, one of the reasons you may have persistent pain or sickness in your body is that there is someone, or a group of people, whom you have not fully forgiven. I don't want to sound harsh, but if that is true and nothing changes on your part, you will remain in your pain and sickness. The wonderful truth is that a short simple prayer of forgiveness from your heart sets you free. Forgiving unlocks the chains of pain in which Satan has you bound.

Forgiveness for some may be very hard, as you may have been terribly abused or taken advantage of. I understand that. God also understands. He stood by while your sin and my sin were put on Jesus. He stood by as Jesus was tortured before the cross. He watched while Jesus slowly suffocated to death on the cross. God chose to forgive each of us for what we did to his Son. Satan wants you to hold on to the grievance. But God would say that there is only one way out: to give your enemies a gift they don't deserve, your forgiveness. When you forgive, you pass them to Father God for him to deal with them. He is a perfect, just, and gracious God who knows far better than we do how to respond to the situation.

Some of you know whom you need to forgive, some of you don't. For those of you who don't, ask the Lord to reveal who it is. It may be that it is more than one person. It could be an organization, a company, or a nation. God loves you and wants you free. He will reveal the key to your healing to you. Make a godly choice today to forgive. It is your key to wholeness and health. Let me lead you through a prayer of forgiveness:

Father, today I choose to forgive _____ (name of the person or people)
I forgive them for what they did to me _____ (be specific about what happened.)

I release them from any further responsibility for what happened to me. I turn them over to you to be the judge and jury in this situation. I offer them a gift that in my opinion they don't deserve. I choose to bless them today. Father would you bless them in their relationships, their health, their finances, and their relationship with you. I thank you Father that you have forgiven me many, many times, and I now forgive

_____ (name of the person or people) .

Let me pray now for you:

> *Father, based on my friend's prayer, I pronounce them forgiven. 1 John*
> *1:9 says that you will now come and cleanse them of all unrighteous-*
> *ness. I bless you Father to wash away every effect of unforgiveness in*
> *their bodies. Father, thank you that their simple prayer is a powerful*
> *prayer that brings healing to them. In the name of Jesus I pray, amen.*

Because forgiveness is such a key part to your healing, I'd like to recommend another book to you. It is called *Grace and Forgiveness* and is written by John and Carol Arnott. You can ask for this at your local Christian bookstore or find it online.

THE POWER OF CONFESSION

There is an incredible power that comes to us when we confess our sins. Confession is good for us; it sets us free from whatever it is that holds us in bondage.

James clearly linked healing to confession when he wrote *"Therefore confess your sins to each other and pray for each other so that you may be healed"* (James 5:16). He did this knowing that Jesus often talked to people about their sin. To the woman who was caught in adultery, he said, *"Go now and leave your life of sin"* (John 8:11).

Luke 5 records the story of the four friends who brought a paralytic to Jesus, at a private meeting in a full house with Pharisees and teachers of the Law.

These ingenious friends burrowed a hole through the roof large enough to lower their paralyzed friend into the room. Do you remember what Jesus reaction was? Luke 5:20 says that Jesus said, *"Friend, your sins are forgiven."* It would appear that Jesus made the link between this man's paralyzed state and his sins. There is no record, but it is very possible that this man was talking to Jesus as he is lowered. Perhaps he was saying something like: "Jesus, I sinned. Please forgive me!" We won't know until we get to heaven, but once there you will find out that I was right!

This isn't the only time that Jesus made a link between sin and sickness. In John 5 Jesus encounters a lame man by the pool called Bethesda. He ministers to the man and when he meets him later in the day Jesus speaks to him about sin: *"See, you are well again. Stop sinning or something worse may happen to you"* (John 5:14).

TAKING OFFENSE SIDETRACKS US!

Many people take offense when someone suggests that their pain or sickness is a result of sin. Can I encourage you that if someone says this kind of thing to you, even rudely, that they may be seeking to help you rather than hurt you. Don't take offense and get sidetracked. Seize the opportunity to ask God to reveal to you if what they are saying is true. If the Father says yes, then ask him to open your eyes to your sin, and confess it.

Several years ago I was ministering with Jim Paul, who pastors in Hamilton, Ontario. We were together in Norwich, England, ministering at a conference. At the end of the meeting, a large group gathered to pray for a blind lady, who was also crippled. It was clear that the Holy Spirit was strongly present, and the group was expecting and hoping for a miracle. Jim, who is very prophetic and also a seer, stood back watching. At one point Jim went to the lady and whispered something in her ear. She shot out of her chair in fear. She turned and looked straight at Jim and said, "How did you know?" Jim, through the Holy Spirit, had just had a revelation of what had caused her blindness and he confronted her with the specifics. The rest of us had no idea what was going on, only that it was very dramatic.

Jim talked to her privately again and each time we heard the same response from the lady. "No!" When she said no the second time, she fell to the floor again blind and lame. She was healed only for 30 seconds! As it turned out, she was unwilling to confess her sin, even though Jim had accurately whispered it to her in private. We later found out from one of the pastors that this lady had an affair and the morning after woke up blind and crippled. Her sin had immediate negative consequences. I think the Holy Spirit was wooing her back. When Jim spoke an accurate diagnosis, she had the option of acknowledging her sin and confessing it, or staying in her sin. Sadly, she stayed in her sin. I know that God is the God of second chances and I'm sure he would allow her another opportunity to repent. I trust she will make a better choice!

SIN ALWAYS HAS CONSEQUENCES

There are never innocent parties when sin is active. James knew this to be true of his congregation. When he wrote about healing, he purposely included confession as a key component. He would have done this because he knew the power of confession. He had seen it in the ministry of Jesus and probably in his own ministry. It would appear that Jesus also taught his disciples this truth. When they encountered a blind man they asked Jesus, *"Rabbi, who sinned, this man or his parents, that he was born blind?"* (John 9:2).

Can I encourage you to ask the Lord for clarity as to the reason you have sickness? Please don't take offense at this, but understand that unconfessed sin limits God from doing the very thing you want him to do. Let me lead you through a time of examination of your past:

> *Father I ask that you will come and be with my friend as we pray together. I ask Holy Spirit that you would lead us into truth. Please come and reveal the truth to my friend.*

Allow him to speak, perhaps grab a pen and paper and quickly write down your thoughts so you can review them in a moment. Ask the Holy Spirit this question: *Holy Spirit, would you now come and reveal to me the source of my sickness or pain?*

When he speaks, you now have the option of agreeing or disagreeing. If you choose to agree with what the Father reveals, pray this prayer with me:

> *Father, I agree with what you have said. I do confess my sin of ____ (be specific) . I admit my part in this and ask you to forgive me. I renounce all the consequences of my sin, including sickness and pain. I ask that as you forgive me you would heal me of all my diseases. I thank you that you had your son Jesus pay for my sin, so that I don't have to pay for it. I choose not to pay for my sin any longer, but to give it to you, knowing that the payment has already been made. Thank you Father for revealing my sin to me. Thank you for forgiving me and setting me free! Amen.*

THE POWER OF AGREEMENT

The Bible teaches that *"if two of you on earth agree about anything you ask for, it will be done for you by my Father in heaven. For where two or three come together in my name, there am I with them"* (Matthew 18:19-20). Jesus says agreement is a powerful tool to get spiritual results, including your healing. Throughout Scripture, unity releases power to change a situation. What we agree with on earth happens in heaven. When people agree, change happens. God jumps into high gear. He likes that we are in agreement with him and he makes the necessary arrangements on our behalf.

I'd like to focus on the aspect of agreement from our passage in James 5. In verse 16 James says, *"Confess your sins to each other and pray for each other so that you may be healed."* Take note that it is when we confess to *each other* that the promise for healing kicks in. It would appear that unity of purpose forces the hand of God into action. The proviso is that the prayer is *"in my name"* (Matthew 18:20). God isn't obliged to act on whimsical desires or selfish requests.

This then brings us back to one of the big questions: Does God want people healed? I say yes, a thousand times yes! So it would seem to me that when two or more people agree on the healing of a person, that we can confidently say that we are asking in the name of Jesus.

God is in the unity business. When people get married they become one. We read in Acts 4:32 about how church is to function: *"All the believers were one in heart and mind. No one claimed that any of his possessions was his own, but they shared everything they had."* The very next verse says, *"With great power the apostles continued to testify to the resurrection of the Lord Jesus, and much grace was upon them all."*

Do you see the connection here? Unity in the church brought great power in ministry.

> *Make every effort to keep the unity of the Spirit through the bond of peace. There is one body and one Spirit; just as you were called to one hope when you were called; one Lord, one faith, one baptism, one God and Father of all, who is over all and through all and in all.* **EPHESIANS 4:3-6**

Satan, on the other hand, is all about division. He hates *oneness* and seeks to cause division between couples, families, churches, countries, businesses, etc. He knows that unity brings power to accomplish tasks and to see prayers answered. He also knows that disunity brings bondage, fear, sickness, and disease.

WHERE DOES SATAN'S POWER COME FROM?

Did you know that there is also a negative power of agreement? The Bible clearly teaches that Satan has been defeated and disarmed (Colossians 2:14-15). So how is it that he is the god of this age? Here is how it works: when Satan deceives a person into agreeing with him, they empower him at that very moment. When Satan tricked Eve into eating the forbidden fruit, she instantly empowered Satan.

On a side note: Adam was standing beside Eve at the time she was being deceived and did nothing. By not stepping in and warning his wife, he also agreed with Satan. Adam is credited in 1 Corinthians 15:22 as bringing sin into our world, not Eve.

In James' practical book for the church family and subsequent followers of Jesus, he shared this simple principle of agreement. He saw the unity that his stepbrother Jesus had with God. He obviously noticed how everything that Jesus did was in tune with the Father. James realized that we can also experience that when we agree with the purposes of God. It seems God is making healing so easy and accessible, that all we need is one person to stand with us and our healing will come!

John and Carol Arnott have seen a number of dramatic miracles. Some of them have been made into docudramas, where people re-enact the healing while telling their stories. They make great videos to give to friends who are skeptical about healing.

One of those videos is the story of Ronnie and Clarice Holden. The Holdens are very successful business people who live in the Carolinas. One night a drunk driver changed everything. Ronnie was seriously injured from the accident with no hope for recovery. His life hung in the balance while Clarice fought against overwhelming odds and tried to find someone to agree with her in prayer. Her Christian doctor didn't think he'd pull through and said he would not agree. After pleading with him, he relented and said he would agree for Ronnie's healing.

Because you can watch the video, I won't tell the whole story other than to say that Ronnie is alive today because of the power of agreement. Clarice faced person after person who didn't believe that God was going to do a miracle for her dying husband. Finally, one person stood with her! You can find this DVD series online.

I have new understanding of why Jesus put his disciples in pairs when he sent them out to minister (Matthew 10). I get why it is not good for a man to be alone; men need someone who will stand with them and agree. I understand the power of the Trinity—it is God agreeing with himself.

My wife often can tell when I am talking to myself. It's not so much that my lips move, but my hands do. Sandra will ask what I'm thinking. My favourite answer is that I'm talking to myself because I need expert advice! Basically, talking to yourself is a form of agreement. We get empowered by hearing ourselves decide on a subject or course of action.

AGREEING FOR A WHEELCHAIR MIRACLE

Several years ago Sandra and I were hosting the Friday night session of a healing conference at our church. We decided to take it seriously, so we skipped the Thursday night session to be with God and listen for his agenda. We listened to quiet music, read our bibles, and journaled.

At one point I felt the Holy Spirit say that we were to find a person in a wheelchair and minister healing to them. Sandra felt the person was going to be a woman, someone we didn't yet know. I felt that she was going to be wearing white. We got a clear sense that God wanted us to find a new lady, wearing white, and get her out of her wheelchair—we agreed!

During worship the next night, Sandra and I talked to some experts on our prayer team. We told a discerner what our plan was. We talked to a deliverance specialist. We found a person with a large gift of faith. All of them agreed with us and said that they would be a part of the team to see a great miracle. Now to find the lady.

As worship continued, I walked through the auditorium. I can't remember exactly how many people there were, but our room can hold up to three thousand and it was almost full. Generally, people in a wheelchair are at the end of a row; sure enough, I saw a lady I'd never seen before who was wearing white. I walked by and had Sandra do the same. We agreed. Next we wanted the lady to agree. I talked to her and explained what we felt to do. Would she allow us to pray for her at the front of the room once the worship time was over? Yes. Great, we were all in agreement!

Well, worship finished and Sandra and I got up; we welcomed the folks to the conference and told them that we were going to demonstrate how easy it was to get people out of wheelchairs. We wanted to create a bit of shock, and I think that did it. What the conference didn't see was the work that we had done behind the scenes to get to that point. We called up our team: the faith person, the discerner, and the deliverance specialist.

I began to interview the lady to get to the root of her situation. We started ministering and within a few minutes the pain left. Then a minute or so later, she felt strength. We had her try standing and she could. After some more prayer we asked her if she wanted to try walking a few steps with assistance. She did it! We asked her if she wanted to try walking with no assistance. She did it! She walked around the auditorium by her self.

Did I mention there was a lot of cheering and encouragement? So how did this miracle take place? Agreement! Find someone who will stand with you. If you don't have another person to stand with you, I'd like to be that person. There are no excuses that are good enough to keep you from being healed. The will of God is clear: God wants us healed! So on that basis, let me agree with you for your healing:

> *Father God, the two of us are agreeing today for my friend's healing.*
> *Father, based on what you inspired James to write, we stand together.*
> *Come and bring healing to my friend's body. Take away all pain, all*
> *sickness, and all diseases. Father we thank you that when we agree*
> *on anything, we touch heaven. We ask that you would hear our prayer*
> *and begin to act. I thank you for my friend's healing today. In the name*
> *of Jesus, amen!*

DOCTORS AND HEALING

Does going to a doctor show a lack of faith? Am I, as a believer in Jesus, allowed to take medicine? Lots of people live under tremendous guilt because they do see doctors and take medicine. In my opinion, you are welcome to do this. Luke, one of the writers of two New Testament books, was a doctor, so that counts for something.

I think I can prove to you, from a Biblical standpoint, that it is okay to use medicine and see physicians. While saying that it is okay, let me begin by stating that I believe God wants you to be healed. I also believe that you should always ask God for your healing, certainly before you head to a physician or begin to take pills. Give God the first opportunity to heal you. I think that those of you who pray for healing and then feel the need to visit a doctor because your pain or sickness persists should do so. God wants you to be well and if a doctor can help, I believe God is happy.

Sadly I do know some who have more faith in doctors and pills than in God's power to heal. I know people who think I am crazy when I don't immediately take a painkiller if I have a headache. I know Christians who don't believe that healing is for today and who would rather take a pill than let someone pray for them. The opposite is also true. Some believers will make fun and jest with people who prefer not to seek medical advice. There are those who believe God has spoken to them to wait in faith for their healing. We've seen news stories of parents who have been charged with involuntary murder because they didn't take their child to a doctor in the name of their faith.

WHO FUNCTIONED AS DOCTORS IN THE BIBLE?

In Matthew 8, Jesus healed a leper and then told him to visit a priest. What's up with that? In the time of Jesus the Levitical law was still enforced. If you had leprosy and thought you were healed you went to see the priest for an examination. You would return seven days later for a follow-up, and if you came back healthy you were pronounced healed and restored to the community. If it looked like your disease had returned, you remained segregated from society.

Today, we don't go to priests or pastors for confirmation that our diseases have been cured, we see doctors. I personally think that if Jesus were here today he would have sent the leper to the local clinic or hospital for a confirmation that a miracle had been performed. I believe that this is what Jesus wanted: an independent confirmation so that glory would be given to God for the healing. Doctors know they don't heal; they simply prescribe, treat, and aid what God wants, your healing.

Can I also suggest that this leper would also be making a statement to the priest? It would have been the priest who would first say, "You have leprosy." A similar statement to "you have cancer" from a doctor. For the priest to see the leper cured would give opportunity for testifying to the goodness of God! In our society, not seeing a doctor when you are sick is seen as foolish by most. If you have a sick child and don't take them to a doctor, you may even run the risk of been seen as a danger to your child. The rights of a child to have medical attention apparently are greater than for the parent to make that decision. Jesus, knowing this man was healed, still followed the customs of his society. He didn't say, "You don't need to go to the doctor, head home right away." He knew the code of conduct for leprosy that the Bible teaches in Leviticus.

Several doctors have told me that their profession often puts them in the place of playing God. One doctor I spoke to in Chicago recently told me that he felt his profession was one of the darkest there is in terms of the low number who have faith in Jesus. Sandra and I were just with an Elim Church in Camberwell, England, with Pastors Sam and Sophie Larbie. Their church is mostly comprised of Africans. Very few people in the congregation are sick. They have seen so many healings that it has to be one of the healthiest churches I've ever been to. Many folks gave testimony to us of spectacular healings. In fact, the churches Sam pastors are growing as people come specifically to be healed, and then they join the congregation.

Many people are looking for alternatives to traditional medicine. They have read the books and seen the reports of how sick our medical system is. There are lots of conspiracy theories out there regarding health, such as pharmaceutical companies trying to keep you alive on pills for the rest of your life, or doctors wanting to operate on you so that the mechanics and function of hospitals keeps going. There are clearly battles between organized medicine and holistic practitioners.

Imagine going to your doctor and hearing a diagnosis that you have cancer. What normally happens is that people take ownership of the diagnosis. They hold the doctor's statement as the ultimate truth and that's when fear begins to set in.

What if we begin to seek a second opinion from the true Healer and take hold of his truth? What an opportunity for you to return cancer-free to your doctor. Your body is a testimony of the fact that God heals time and time again.

A DOCTOR GETS HER HEALING

There are many doctors and health providers who attend our church. In fact, at one point I think we had close to ten doctors on our prayer ministry team helping to minister to sick people. One of the specialists at our church is Stephanie. She is a sports chiropractor who specializes with elite athletes. In 2011, Stephanie was diagnosed with an unexpected brain tumor. Stephanie is young and this was not good news. She took time to listen to God and felt him say not to get treatment. She had complete faith that he would take care of her. Imagine a doctor telling her colleagues that she was not going to have radiation or any other form of medicine to cure this life-threatening challenge.

Stephanie's fiancé, Anthony (they are now married), is also is a doctor. He too specializes with elite athletes and his focus is imaging, as in MRIs, X-rays, etc. Anthony is so good that for several Olympics he ran the imaging department of the athletes' hospital. Anthony was one of the doctors to confirm to Stephanie that she did indeed have a brain tumor. Anthony was also in agreement with her about her plan and encouraged Stephanie to receive prayer. We talked and I encouraged him to bring Stephanie to our Catch The Fire conference that was the next week.

They took a day off work and came to a couple sessions on the Friday. I remember seeing Stephanie standing on a prayer line and ministering to her. She told me afterwards that she felt something change. Great! That night Heidi Baker was ministering. Heidi did something unusual, in that she invited all the medical people at the conference to come to the front. Stephanie and Anthony were at the front as Heidi began to minister. Stephanie again felt something happen to her that was dramatic and powerful. She had great hope that God had done something in her body!

A few days later I got an excited phone call from Anthony on a Monday morning. He was at the hospital having just taken another MRI of Stephanie's brain. The news was unbelievable: the tumor had died and was shriveling up. Stephanie shared this story herself at one of our meetings. Imagine this: a medical doctor decides not to have medical treatment for a serious, life-threatening disease. She obeys God and gets her healing and has pictures to prove it. I love it!

Please don't be afraid of seeing specialists. Doctors and specialists are not the final word, God is. In fact, I think that the medical practitioners on our prayer team have an advantage. They know in the natural what has to happen for a healing to take place. They know which nerve has to be restored. They know which organ is causing a symptom. They know how this disease causes pain. They can pray and minister with more focus and I believe with more authority.

Is God able to use the wisdom of a financial advisor to help you balance your budget? Is God able to use the skill of an architect when you want to build your own home? God is also able to use doctors to help you. Don't be afraid to see them! In his book *Kisses From A Good God*, Paul Manwaring, of Bethel Church in Redding, California, describes how God healed him of prostate cancer, using a surgeon and a scalpel. Thank you Lord for our doctors!

MEDICINE IN THE BIBLE

Let's talk about medicine for a bit. God is not afraid to heal people in many different ways. Jesus didn't have one technique for healing. The Bible tells of us three specific blind people having their eyes restored and each one was different. Mud, spit and a touch; all apparently effective!

King Hezekiah was dying and a prophet came to him. God gave him fifteen extra years to live. How did God heal him? He was asked to eat figs! Not a touch from a prophet, not baptize yourself in the Jordan seven times, not anything spiritual (2 Kings 20:6-7).

In the New Testament, Paul writes to Timothy and at one point addresses his weak stomach. Paul doesn't say a prayer for him, he tells him to drink wine (1 Timothy 5:23). His recommendation was a treatment, not a divine healing. Interesting.

As we see in the Old Testament writings, God gave the Jewish people very strict laws on how to live. Many laws were related to how they worshipped and how they dealt with other nations. A huge amount of rules were given for their diet, washing, sexual relationships, etc. Food such as pork, lobster, shrimp, and catfish were on the do not eat list. Jesus clearly changed the rules when he declared all foods clean (Mark 7:19). So, we can now eat all the lobster we want? Well, this is where another scripture comes in. Paul wrote in 1 Corinthians 6:12 and 10:23 that everything is allowable (as Jesus said), but not everything is beneficial or constructive for us.

As may you know, most of the food items in the no-go list from the Old Testament are actually not healthy ones. Pork takes far more energy to digest that most other meats. Lobster and shrimp come with high cholesterol content and hinder the health of your heart. So, although we have liberty to eat anything we want, we need restraint and wisdom. God knew this and was seeking to keep people from getting sick. God was doing the pre-emptive work so that people didn't need to be healed later on. All the studies of food intake tell us that Western diets are the least healthy. Western people also tend to break the dietary codes of the Old Testament the most!

Sandra and I recently led a group of 82 people to Israel. I don't know how we got onto the subject but one of our tour guides talked to us about health issues. We were talking about the Orthodox Jews and he said that these women never have "lady" problems. Okay, why? His answer was that they follow the rules of Leviticus when it comes to times of the month when they don't have sex as married couples. Did God actually make a way for women to stay healthy? Was God being preventative? While I know the Bible is not primarily a health and lifestyle book, nor a cookbook, it does record God's wisdom and we would be wise to heed the warnings and code of conduct that is contained in it.

If you are feeling guilt or condemnation over seeing doctors or taking medicine, let me minister to you now:

> *Father, I thank you that Jesus sent the leprous man to the priest. Father, you are the one who gives wisdom and insight and through the years you have allowed doctors and health workers to understand much of how you bring healing.*

> *Father, I lift off all false guilt, condemnation, and fear of doctors or of going to doctors. I command anything that is not from you to go quietly to the cross. I bless doctors to help my friend in the healing process. We thank you Father that you want us well. If you choose to use medicine,*

we are okay with that. We thank you that your heart is for us to be free from pain and all illness.

Father, may our bodies be a wonderful testimony of your touch. May we have opportunities to share what you have done in our bodies with those in the medical profession. Father, heal our bodies, however you choose to do it. In the name of Jesus, amen.

ONE LAST WORD

Friends I trust what some of what I have written in this book has challenged you. You do not need to agree with me on all or even some points. My purpose in writing was twofold: First, to convince you that God wants people well. I trust I did that. Second, for you to know how easy and rewarding it is to bring healing to another person. Now that you've finished the book, it is time to step up and step out. Begin to act with greater revelation! Begin to minister with great anointing! One last prayer, if I may:

Father, thank you for my friend and their diligence in reading this book. Anoint them to levels that they have not yet experienced. Father, for those who need healing, may they be healed as they say this prayer:

My healing belongs to me,
Because of what Jesus has done.
I receive my healing, now! Amen!

ABOUT THE AUTHOR

Steve Long is the senior leader of Catch The Fire Toronto. When the Toronto Blessing began in 1994, Steve and his wife Sandra joined in as participants and soon became leaders. Steve is a classic Bible teacher who loves to tell stories of what God is doing in people's lives. Along with providing leadership for the Toronto church, Steve and Sandra also travel and minister around the world. Steve is an avid sports enthusiast who is currently training his grandsons to be athletes to provide for his pension!

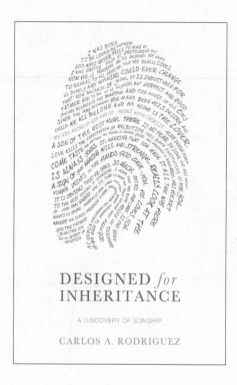

DESIGNED FOR INHERITANCE

CARLOS A. RODRIGUEZ

With personal stories, practical teaching and deep revelation, *Designed For Inheritance* is a fresh invitation to encounter true love Himself. A call to hear clearly from the only voice that can define you. As you receive the embrace that will change your life, you will discover the unimaginable realities of your sonship and inheritance.

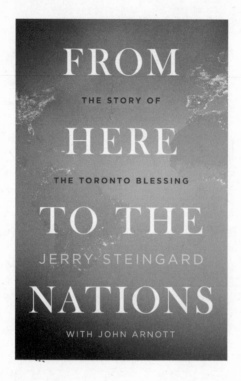

FROM HERE TO THE NATIONS

JERRY STEINGARD • JOHN ARNOTT

In 1994, the power of God fell on a little church at the end of a runway in Toronto. *From Here To The Nations* tells the remarkable story of what would come to be called The Toronto Blessing, and the incredible impact it has had on the church over the last 20 years. Step inside the doors of Catch The Fire, and read the full story from a close observer and participant. Let thankfulness arise as you hear the amazing stories of the Father's love, and let your spirit soar as you hear the prophecies for the next tsunami wave of revival!

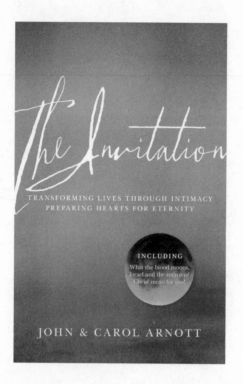

THE INVITATION

JOHN & CAROL ARNOTT

In their latest book, John and Carol Arnott share both biblical and personal revelation of the importance of investing in intimacy with God in preparation for the return of Jesus. Whether you are a leader, a church member or a new believer, *The Invitation* will inspire you to to take practical steps today which are fundamental in preparing your heart for the Lord's return. Building a life of intimacy with God will bring transformation into every area of your life. There is no time left to be lukewarm.

S CATCH THE FIRE | COLLEGE

If you want to take the next step in living
a supernatural life then Catch The Fire's
Leaders Schools are exactly what you need.

Our Leaders Schools are three weeks away from the demands of life
and ministry to encounter God in a new way. The intention of these
schools is to renew and refresh leaders and to allow them to pursue
greater intimacy and deeper relationship with him. We want you to
experience the love of the father and have your heart restored.

The Leaders Schools are specially designed for ministers, lay leaders,
leaders in business and communities, missionaries and spouses. It is
a safe place where you can take time out from ministry and find new
passion, vision and direction for your life.

For more information visit **catchthefire.com/college**

The DAY you were Born
is The DAY God Dicided
That The world could
Not exist without you

Very good